THE THRONE, THE LAMB & THE DRAGON

Paul Spilsbury

A READER'S GUIDE TO THE BOOK OF REVELATION

Foreword by J. I. Packer

IVP Academic

An imprint of InterVarsity Press
Downers Grove, Illinois

InterVarsity Press
P.O. Box 1400, Downers Grove, IL 60515-1426
World Wide Web: www.ivpress.com
E-mail: mail@ivpress.com

©2002 by Paul Spilsbury

InterVarsity Press® is the book-publishing division of InterVarsity Christian Fellowship/USA®, a student movement active on campus at hundreds of universities, colleges and schools of nursing in the United States of America, and a member movement of the International Fellowship of Evangelical Students. For information about local and regional activities, write Public Relations Dept., InterVarsity Christian Fellowship/USA, 6400 Schroeder Rd., P.O. Box 7895, Madison, WI 53707-7895, or visit the IVCF website at < www.intervarsity.org >.

Scripture quotations are from the New Revised Standard Version *of the Bible, copyright 1989 by the Division of Christian Education of the National Council of the Churches of Christ in the USA. Used by permission. All rights reserved.*

Cover illustration: Roberta Polfus

ISBN-10: 0-8308-2671-8
ISBN-13: 978-0-8308-2671-1

Printed in the United States of America ∞

Library of Congress Cataloging-in-Publication Data

Spilsbury, Paul, 1966-
    The throne, the lamb & the dragon: a reader's guide to the Book of Revelation/Paul Spilsbury.
    p. cm.
    Includes bibliographical references.
    ISBN 0-8308-2671-8 (pbk.)
    1. Bible. N.T. Revelation—Criticism, interpretation, etc. I. Title: Throne, the lamb, and the dragon. II. Title.

BS2825.2 .S69 2002
228'.06—dc21

                         2001051797

P	23	22	21	20	19	18	17	16	15	14	13	12	11	10	9	8	7	6	5	4	3
Y	24	23	22	21	20	19	18	17	16	15	14	13	12	11	10	09	08	07			

For Elliot and Oliver

CONTENTS

FOREWORD BY J. I. PACKER   9

PREFACE   11

1. READING REVELATION   15

2. HOLDING IT TOGETHER   41

3. THE THRONE   51

4. THE LAMB   67

5. THE DRAGON   89

6. WRATH & JUDGMENT   109

7. NO MORE TEARS   129

EPILOGUE   149

SUGGESTIONS FOR FURTHER READING   154

INDEX   156

Foreword

The Revelation to John is a visionary circular to churches in Asia Minor that announces itself as a book of prophecy. Basic to it are the seven letters of assessment, admonition and encouragement that the Lord Jesus dictated to John, and that now make up chapters 2 and 3. Each letter ends with a promise of ultimate glory for everyone who "overcomes" in the approaching conflicts. Next comes a long series of visions—by turns fantastic, grotesque, horrific and sublime—in which all Christians are martyrs, all humanity tastes God's wrath, and all the beauties of new heaven, new earth and new Jerusalem are outlined. Hymns of praise hold it all together in a kaleidoscope that is as deeply devotional as it is disturbing.

This is an apocalypse, of a kind that Jewish imaginations—Scripture-soaked, theologically fueled, disaster-driven—were producing long before Christ. It is a picture book in which all the pictures are theological symbols, and some are pictures explaining other pictures. Since we do not write such works today, interpreting Revelation became a sort of Christian puzzle corner, especially in the West where dispensational hermeneutics and millennial dreams made the brew headier.

But that should now be a thing of the past.

Older interpreters would identify "the scarlet woman" with the papacy, and from there work back over past history and forward to some form of millennium. Such views still exist. But scholarship has moved into a new era of apocalyptic appreciation, and Paul Spilsbury has creamed off much of its wisdom to nourish ordinary Bible lovers. His work delights me, and not just because he is a former student of mine; he has got the hang of the book, and is on the right track with it all the way. (Whether I agree with every sentence is neither here nor there.) There are huge benefits to be gained from what he has written, and I heartily commend it.

J. I. Packer

Preface

When I was asked to teach the book of Revelation several years ago, I took up the task with more than the normal degree of fear and trepidation. Revelation, after all, has a reputation for being a difficult and controversial book. Now I had to come to terms with it myself, as well as explain it to others. As the semester progressed, though, I found myself deeply moved by this astonishing document. Its vivid scenes and powerful language were far more exciting than I was expecting. Anticipating a book of dark riddles and impenetrable mysteries, I discovered instead a clear and pointed message.

I found, first of all, that Revelation is a book about God, the One who sits on the throne of the universe and is surrounded by the eternal worship of the heavenly host. Just who God is and what it means to worship him are the issues at the heart of Revelation's message. Second, I discovered that Revelation is a book about Jesus, the Lamb who was slaughtered and whose death and resurrection make God's kingdom a reality on earth. Revelation also makes clear that those who want to follow the Lamb are called not only to continue his work in the world but also to share his experience of suffering. We will share in his victory, certainly, but not before we have shared in his death. This is one of Revelation's most pointed challenges. Third, I found that Revelation is a book about a terrible conflict. Here is a story of mortal combat between "the One who sits on the throne" and his archenemy, the dragon. Those who worship God and follow the Lamb are embroiled in this conflict whether they like it or not. Indeed, this conflict is the very context of their lives.

In what follows I seek to distill the broad message of Revelation, not to explain or discuss every verse of the book. This is an essay on what Revelation is about and a guide on how to read it—the "big picture," rather than the details. I want to open up to a wider public the best of what biblical scholars have been saying about Revelation in recent times. Indeed, I am deeply indebted to many of them for my understanding of this book. Richard Bauckham's *The Theology of the Book of Revelation* deserves special mention. Readers who want to expand what they learn in the following pages would do well to start with him. Additionally, I urge them to consult the "Suggestions for Further Reading" at the end of this volume.

Many people have supported me by offering guidance and encouragement throughout the writing of this book, and I am only too happy to record my indebtedness and gratitude to them. I am very grateful to Prof. John Barclay of the University of Glasgow, who read and commented insightfully on the manuscript in the midst of his own very busy schedule. Dr. Daniel G. Reid of InterVarsity Press and Prof. David deSilva of Ashland Theological Seminary also read the entire manuscript and provided a wealth of assistance. (Of course the remaining shortcomings of this book are mine, not theirs.) I also want to acknowledge the contributions of the students at Canadian Bible College in Regina and at Regent College in Vancouver who have attended my lectures on Revelation in one form or another. Their questions and probing have sharpened my understanding of Revelation and given an increased urgency to the writing of this book. Marcia Hinds upheld me with her prayers and timely insights, for which I am indeed thankful. My wife and ally in life, Bronwyn Spilsbury, gave many hours to making this book much more readable and coherent than it would otherwise have been. I am deeply grateful to her. Finally, I dedicate this book to our two sons, Elliot and Oliver, who are a source of great joy and pride to their parents. May they, along with us all, learn to follow the Lamb wherever he goes.

1

READING REVELATION

Revelation is not a book for the faint-hearted. Its message is deeply disturbing. It unsettles us. It urges us to reevaluate the most fundamental of our convictions, our loyalties and commitments. What are our true values? What is really the most important thing in our lives? What would we be willing to die for? What does the evidence of our daily lives say about who we really are? These are the kinds of questions Revelation urges us to ask ourselves. As I said, Revelation is not a book for the faint-hearted.

At its most basic level Revelation calls us to worship God. When all the terrible sights have passed us by and the sulphurous smoke has settled, one image must remain with us: there is One who sits on the throne. He sits in luminous splendor, surrounded by mighty celestial beings who continually cry, "Holy, holy, holy, the Lord God the Almighty, who was and is and is to come." And at his feet the entire created order falls down and shouts, "You are worthy, our Lord and God, to receive glory and honor and power, for you created all things, and by your will they existed and were created." This is the One on whom the vision focuses, the One whom Revelation calls us to adore. Only God is truly real in a world of mirages and illusions.

The book of Revelation also calls us to follow Jesus Christ, portrayed as a slaughtered lamb. His way is the way of suffering, the way of sacrifice. It is the way of salvation, yes; it is the way to glory, certainly; but it leads us through defeat, dereliction and death. In the book of Revelation those who follow the Lamb "follow him wherever he goes," and they "wash their robes and make them white in the blood of the Lamb." These terms speak of our joining with Christ in a life marked by his character and his experience. If we were following a superhero we might have expected to live like mini superheroes. But our savior is not a superhero. He is the Lamb who was slain. This fact forever determines the nature of true discipleship: those who follow Jesus must be like him.

Revelation also tells us that those who follow the Lamb follow him into an unequal battle. On the one side is the Lamb and his followers dressed in white robes and carrying palm branches—hardly the garb of war. On the other side is a terrifying seven-headed dragon. This dragon (an image of Satan himself) also has backup forces: a sea beast and a land monster working like a diabolical tag-team. Together this evil trinity disputes the claims of the One who sits on the throne, and by their deceitfulness they lead the world to its destruction. Their only opponents, the only ones who can stop their evil work, are the Lamb and his followers—who have no weapons besides their faithful and true witness to the reality of the One who sits on the throne. And so the conflict revolves around who the true God is. Who has the right to receive the worship of the universe?

Shockingly, the book of Revelation chronicles the *defeat* of the Lamb and his followers, slain at the hands of the evil trio. Yet their defeat is the essence of their ultimate victory, because God's rule is energized not by brute force but by what Paul in a different context referred to as "power made perfect in weakness." Although they are slain, ultimately they overcome evil; in the end they enter through the twelve gates of the New Jerusalem that comes down out of heaven. This is the final victory, for the New Jerusalem is the place of God's unmediated presence, the place where God is truly worshipped and the world's evil no longer exists. Here, in one of biblical literature's most powerful and enduring visions of human hope, God wipes away every tear and there is no more death.

These are the broad strokes of the picture Revelation presents us. But we are getting ahead of ourselves, because we must acknowledge that Revelation is a difficult book to understand, sometimes even a difficult book to stomach—more people are killed or struck down with disease than in any other biblical book. There are more calamities, more disasters, more horrors and terrors. On top of all that, the book is an enigma—as if it were written in code or a language we do not understand. We tend to avoid things that make us feel ignorant, clueless and inadequate. And that is often how we feel with Revelation, not just when we read the book for ourselves but perhaps even more when we hear people confidently expounding on how this or that current event is clearly a fulfillment of this or that verse in Revelation. As a result many of us have tended quietly to avoid the book altogether. Some of us might even own up to a certain sense of embarrassment about it all and wish that the Bible ended with a rousing benediction from the apostle Paul rather than this mysterious and troubling vision.

Yet for all that, we know we cannot ignore this book. We sense instinctively that Revelation contains something of great value if only we could discover it. As the last book of the Bible it has a special significance; it is a kind of climax or grand finale to the biblical story. No one likes to abandon an epic just a few pages before the end. Knowing how it all turns out is vital for our understanding of the book as a whole.

In addition, Revelation starts off by pronouncing a blessing on its readers: "Blessed is the one who reads aloud the words of the prophecy, and blessed are those who hear and who keep what is written in it; for the time is near" (1:3). Not many other books of the Bible can boast anything similar. It is as if this book has been singled out for our attention, and we need this extra encouragement to press on despite the difficulties and our sense of inadequacy.

But the promise implies that those who read have sufficient understanding to put into practice the things learned from the book—and that is where we stumble. How can we "keep what is written" if we can hardly grasp what the book is trying to say to us? We need guidance about how to read Revelation so we can receive the blessing it promises.

That guidance is what I hope to provide in this book. With just a few general principles in place, Revelation can become much less daunting and more approachable. I do not say less frightening, because Revelation remains a disturbing book. But the fear it induces is not a cringing or paranoid fear. Rather, Revelation issues the very same invitation and warning as the Gospels—to enter into the kingdom of God while counting the cost and facing the challenges of being a disciple of the crucified one.

To understand Revelation, to gain access to the inner secrets of its vision, we must ask the right questions. In the case of Revelation, the first and most fundamental question is: What kind of book is this? Is Revelation an outline of history, as some have thought? Is it a parable or an allegory? Is it a literal description of the future, like a history book written in advance of the events? Is it a sermon written in some kind of secret code? Or is it simply something beyond us, something we will never fully understand? These questions, which are actually questions about the literary *genre* of Revelation, help us come to grips with what makes Revelation tick. Asking what kind of literature it is gets us right into the heart of the book, so we will need to give this question a careful answer.

The Genre of the Book of Revelation
The question about what kind of book Revelation is has been answered in lots of ways. Before giving the answer that I think is most helpful, I want to outline some of the answers others have given. The first answer—which has been popular since the book was written—is that Revelation is a kind of

allegorical overview of church history in advance. According
to this theory, called the *historicist* approach, Revelation pre-
dicts different ages or epochs in the church's development.
The seven churches in chapters 2 and 3, for example, are
taken to represent seven consecutive stages in church history, starting with the apostolic church (represented by
Ephesus) and ending with the apostate church about to be
spat out of God's mouth (represented by Laodicea). The various judgments portrayed by the seals, trumpets and bowls
likewise represent significant events down the course of history (for example, the rise of Islam or the papacy).

Such an approach was extremely influential in Europe during the Middle Ages, and continued into recent times with
groups such as the Branch Davidians in Waco, Texas. But it
has several serious problems. First, the people who support
these kinds of theories almost always assume that they themselves are living in the last, or nearly the last, phase of history. Thus, depending on whether their world is medieval
Europe or modern-day America, Revelation has to be
stretched out to differing lengths to make it fit the theory. History, too, has to be summarized in just the right way to make
it fit into Revelation. This produces odd interpretations of
Revelation, and some dubious and strangely stylized accounts
of history. Second, these theories tend to focus on the history
of the church in the western world, as if Christians in Africa
and Asia or anywhere else have no place in God's plan. Perhaps most significantly of all, though, this way of reading Revelation makes the book irrelevant to its original readers. Yet
we know from the fact that Revelation was copied and pre-
served for future generations that those readers did indeed

find it deeply meaningful for their own situations. However we come to read Revelation, we must take into account what those original readers found so powerful in it.

The second answer to the question about Revelation's genre, called the *futurist* approach, is that the book is a prediction of events that will take place in the last few years before the end of the world. Here too the approach is allegorical: characters such as the dragon and the beast, and events such as the plagues and earthquakes, are taken to represent future personages and events. According to this theory, Revelation provides the blueprint for the course of future events, including most significantly the rise of the antichrist, the playing out of the "great tribulation," the "rapture" of the church, the battle of Armageddon and the return of Christ. This way of reading Revelation is especially popular in North America and is perhaps best known in the form popularized by Hal Lindsey during the 1970s and fictionalized in the Left Behind series at the turn of the twenty-first century. However, it suffers from some of the same defects as the first reading. It too makes the book strangely irrelevant to John's first readers, this time by placing a gap of nearly two thousand years (so far!) between the writing of the book and its fulfillment.

The futurist theory has other problems too. It takes no account of the way first-century readers would have understood the book's many images. Thus, a swarm of deadly locusts is more likely to be treated as a squadron of helicopter gunships than in the way we find them understood in the Bible itself (for example, Joel 1:2-18). Indeed, the literary character of Revelation is all but ignored by this way of reading it. Perhaps the weakest aspect of the futurist approach, though, is that those who use it to predict the future never get it right: all their major predictions have failed to materialize. Also, these books are strangely silent about the major events that have indeed occurred in recent times. In the end, this approach to Revelation is simply not reliable. We need to find a better answer to the question of what Revelation is really all about.

The best answers to that question are those that take careful note of the literary characteristics of the book itself. This might sound obvious, but many who try to interpret the book ignore it. When we do take Revelation seriously as a form of ancient literature, we find two basic literary facts that, though mundane, have far-reaching implications for how we read Revelation and what lessons we glean from it. The two facts are these: Revelation is a *letter;* and Revelation is an *apocalypse.* We need to explore each of these.

Revelation Is a Letter

How do we know that Revelation is a letter? First, the document starts in the standard way that ancient letters started. In those days, letter writers would generally introduce themselves by name, say who they were writing to, and add a simple greeting. The standard formula would be something like this: "Bob to Jane, hello!" Of course, there could be variations of this formula. Revelation begins with an expanded form of the standard letter-opening: "John to the seven churches in Asia. Grace and peace to you" (1:4). There are a number of unusual things about the beginning of Revelation, but they don't overturn the fact that we are still dealing with a letter.

Add to this the way the document ends, which is exactly how we would expect an ancient Christian letter to end, and it is beyond doubt that Revelation is a letter.

What is so interesting about this? Well, a letter is a special kind of document that has to be read in an appropriate way. Because letters are so closely connected to specific people, relationships, circumstances and events, we have to take all those things into account if we are to understand their contents. When we get a letter from a friend or acquaintance we take most of this information for granted. For example, we do not make a special effort to place the letter in its historical context because we are a part of that context. But things would be different if we were reading someone else's mail. And that, in effect, is what we are doing when we read ancient letters. What was taken for granted by both the writer and the readers of those letters must now be carefully spelled out.

This means that to understand Revelation we need to know something about the author of the letter and the people it was written to. We also need to know something about the events and circumstances that led to writing the letter. Why did the author write this particular letter at this time and in this manner? What was the letter supposed to accomplish? These are essential questions for a correct reading of the document. The answers will relate directly to how we understand what we read. Remember, as a letter Revelation must have made sense to its original readers. Otherwise why would it have been written to them? Knowing the historical background gives us a better idea of how the original readers would have reacted to and understood the letter. So let me sketch out some basic information about each of the relevant issues.

First of all, the author. He calls himself "John" a number of times (1:1, 4, 9; 22:8). Since this was a fairly common name in first-century Christian circles, what more can we say about him? Clearly he was a Christian prophet. In several places he calls his writing prophecy (1:3; 22:7, 10, 18, 19); an angel says to him: "I am a fellow servant with you and your comrades the prophets" (22:9). Thus John thought of himself, and intended for us to think of him, as someone with a message that had been communicated to him directly from God. This is very significant because in John's day many people believed that the prophets belonged to a golden age already long past. In the fledgling Christian communities, though, there was a new conviction that God was again speaking to his people through specially gifted servants. John was such an individual.

What more do we know about him? Not very much, although the church has always believed that this is the same John who was one of the Twelve, the son of Zebedee and the brother of James. According to early church tradition, this John moved to Ephesus where he became a pastor to the Christian communities in Asia Minor (modern-day western Turkey), and at one point was exiled to the island of Patmos because of his faith. But scholars in more recent times have come to doubt this tradition—not least because the John of Revelation never refers to himself as an apostle or one of the original twelve disciples. Apparently he preferred to be thought of simply as John the prophet. So perhaps we should leave it at that.

The next question relates to the recipients of the letter: the people to whom John wrote. They were Christians living in seven cities about which John was particularly concerned: Ephesus, Smyrna, Pergamum, Thyatira, Sardis, Philadelphia and Laodicea. The gospel arrived in this part of the world as much as half a century before Revelation was written, through the missionary efforts of Paul and other Christians. Therefore, many of the Christians addressed here would have been mature in their faith, with their congregations fairly well established. They were not all doing well spiritually, though, as the book reveals.

The fact that John was writing to seven churches and not just one tells us that Revelation is a kind of circular letter intended for a broad audience. This suggests that the message of the book is fairly wide-ranging. Different people would have heard this letter differently, depending on how they were faring at the time. For those who were progressing well in their Christian faith and practice, the letter would bring encouragement and inspiration. But for those who had grown stale in their faith, or who were compromising their commitment in order to make progress in the world, the message of Revelation was far from encouraging. Rather it was a message of warning and impending judgment.

Something else is also going on here. As we will see later, the number seven has important symbolic value for Revelation. It indicates something like wholeness or completeness. The fact that Revelation addresses precisely seven churches is its way of alerting us to the fact that it is really speaking to the whole church. This is a message to all Christians everywhere, not just to these seven communities. That point is reinforced by the refrain at the end of each message to the churches in chapters 2 and 3: "Let anyone who has an ear lis-

ten to what the Spirit is saying to the churches." In a sense
these seven churches represent a kind of snapshot of the
state of the church at any given time. There will always be
some who are doing well and others who are complacent.
There will always be some who need warm encouragement
while others need a sterner word to get them moving. The
sevenfold message orients us to the main vision that takes up
the rest of the book of Revelation. It primes us for how we
should be listening to what is about to be said. Not everyone
should take a message of encouragement from this vision.
Nor is it a sharp message of impending judgment for all. How
we hear it depends on our state of mind and the condition of
our discipleship at the moment we read it.

Finally, we need to say something about the circumstances that led to the writing of the letter. Scholars debate
two possible dates for the writing of Revelation. The first and
perhaps most widely accepted option is that the book was
written during the reign of the emperor Domitian some time
very close to the end of the first century—probably in the
mid-90s. Domitian was feared and hated even by the highest-
ranking Roman elite (some of them eventually murdered
him). Possibly Christians came under pressure during his
reign to participate in the imperial cult, a form of state religion designed to honor the emperor as divine. Domitian
apparently like to be called "Lord and God," even by senior
Roman officials. While the evidence for widespread persecution of Christians during this time is not strong, Christians
throughout the empire may have feared that Rome was about
to turn very nasty and that they would soon come under
pressure to acknowledge the emperor as God. A number of

passages in Revelation seem to imply such a fear.

The second plausible option is to date the writing of Revelation to a time just after the emperor Nero's death, almost thirty years earlier. This is based on an interpretation of the five fallen kings (17:9-10) as referring to the first five Roman emperors: Augustus, Tiberius, Caligula, Claudius and Nero. Nero's death in A.D. 68 was followed by a period of great political turmoil in Rome, with four individuals struggling for power. Such upheaval may be reflected in some scenes in John's vision.

In either case Revelation was written in a time when Christians were beginning to experience the growing suspicion and hostility of the state. It was not yet a time of universal or systematic persecution, but there was a sense of storm clouds beginning to gather on the horizon. Indeed, John is writing from exile on the island of Patmos and he addresses his readers as those who share with him "the persecution and the kingdom and the patient endurance" (1:9). He also speaks of a certain Antipas who has already been killed for his faithful witness in Pergamum (2:13). To the church in Smyrna Christ counsels: "Do not fear what you are about to suffer. Beware, the devil is about to throw some of you into prison so that you may be tested, and for ten days you will have affliction. Be faithful until death, and I will give you the crown of life" (2:10).

Because Revelation is a letter, we must take seriously all these issues relating to its history. It was written at a particular time to a particular group of people to address particular conditions and circumstances. The original message of the book relates to these historical facts, and its ongoing relevance for us today cannot be cut loose from these original moorings—any more than we can cut off the rest of the Bible from the time and place in which it was written. When we read 1 Corinthians we know that Paul was writing to a specific audience and that both his circumstances and theirs had a direct bearing on what he wrote. We also know that his message is deeply rooted in the life and times of ancient Corinth, so we will need to do a little historical background work if we are to get to the bottom of everything the apostle said to that Christian community.

The same is true of Revelation. John knew the people he was writing to and he wrote to address certain specific spiritual and pastoral needs. He didn't write a document for our benefit alone, any more than Paul wrote 1 Corinthians for us alone. Yet when we treat Revelation as if it were about the events unfolding in our newspapers today, we detach it from its original setting, saying in essence that those first readers were mistaken to think that it was written for them. But the evidence of history is that communities copy and preserve texts that they find helpful and relevant to their own lives. We have Revelation today precisely because its first readers found it to be meaningful for their own situation back then. Our understanding of this text must be based on its original setting—it must be connected to what its original readers thought it was all about.

Revelation Is an Apocalypse

John is clear that the immediate cause of his writing was a visitation from Christ and an experience of being taken into another dimension through a door that opened in the heav-

ens. The visitation from Christ accounts for most of the first
three chapters of the book; the journey into another world
accounts for the next nineteen chapters. The content of
these amazing experiences leads us to consider the second of
the two literary characteristics of Revelation that I mentioned earlier. Revelation is not just a letter—it is also an
example of an ancient literature called *apocalyptic.*

The common feature of apocalyptic literature, which was
well known in Jewish and Christian circles at the time Revelation was written, is that it claims to report a heavenly revelation of some kind (the Greek word *apocalypsis* means
"revelation"). This revelation is usually delivered to a prophet
or visionary by an angel, is given in symbolic form, and
includes highly dramatic events and images. When we read
Revelation we need to keep in mind that we are not reading a
straightforward story. In many ways it is more like a poem,
with its many figures of speech, literary images and metaphors. So we have to make a special effort to understand
what we are reading—more is going on than appears on the
surface.

Some people immediately become uncomfortable with
talk about metaphors and images in Revelation, as if this
somehow undermines the authority of the book. "Don't you
believe it is literal?" they might ask. But none of us believes
that the Lord Jesus is *literally* a lamb, least of all a lamb with
seven eyes! Yet this is how Jesus is depicted in Revelation.
God (who is Spirit) does not literally sit on a throne, as
depicted in chapter 4, and God's "seven spirits" are a symbolic way of referring to the perfection of God's one Spirit.

This general point applies across the board to all the personalities, creatures, actions and events depicted in Revelation. Whether it is stars falling from heaven or armies of locusts invading the earth, we are dealing with symbols and metaphors. Indeed, to read Revelation as a book that uses symbolic language is to read it precisely as it demands to be read. There is no better way to acknowledge and respect the book's authority than that.

We can take this a step further by looking at two examples of how Revelation uses imagery: the Lamb with seven eyes, and the seven spirits of God. Both of these illustrate how Revelation uses symbols: each has a significant number and an image drawn from the Old Testament. We will talk about the numbers first.

Revelation and numbers. Certain numbers are particularly important in the book of Revelation. The number seven (and its multiples) is a prime example: there are seven lamp stands, seven stars, seven spirits of God, seven seals on the scroll and so on. Other significant numbers include twelve (and its multiples), and three, four and ten.

In coming to grips with these numbers we first need to realize that they were deliberately placed in the text in this way—it didn't just happen. Then we must try to understand what they *mean* in the context of Revelation, rather than simply taking them as literal numbers. For example, the number twelve relates easily to the fact that in the Hebrew Bible the people of God consisted of twelve tribes. When Revelation says there are twelve gates into the New Jerusalem, it is not giving us celestial architecture, it is telling us that this is the home of all those who belong to God. The same applies to the number 144,000, which is a multiple of twelve (12 x 12 x

1000). This is a way of talking about the vast company of people who belong to the Lamb. It is not placing a limit on how many true followers of Christ there are.

Returning to the number seven, we find that ancient literature often used it to symbolize perfection or completeness. The ancients believed there were seven planets and seven "wonders"; Genesis speaks of creation being accomplished in seven days. To say that the Lamb had seven eyes is to emphasize Jesus' perfection, not give us a physical description. The same is true of other numbers in Revelation. We need to be careful about them; they have values that go beyond what appears on the surface.

Revelation and the Old Testament. The images of the Lamb and the seven spirits of God also illustrate how Revelation draws on the Old Testament. The slaughtered Lamb is a reminder of ancient Israel's sacrificial system, and especially of that special sacrificial victim, the Passover lamb. Thus, when we read about the Lamb we are supposed to think of what the Old Testament can tell us about who Jesus is and what he has accomplished.

The key to the meaning of the seven spirits is in the book of Zechariah, where the ancient seer relates a vision in which he saw a seven-branched lampstand. In his vision he asks his angelic guide for the meaning of what he has seen, and this is the answer he gets: "This is the word of the Lord . . . not by might, nor by power, but by my spirit says the Lord of hosts" (Zech 4:6). The image of God's Spirit represented by a seven-fold flame is what Revelation wants us to think of when we read: "Coming from the throne are flashes of lightning, and rumblings and peals of thunder,

and in front of the throne burn seven flaming torches, which
are the seven spirits of God" (4:5). The "flaming torches" in
Revelation correspond to the seven lamps in Zechariah's
vision, which in turn correspond to the seven-branched
lampstand that "stood before the LORD" in the Israelite tabernacle (Ex 37:17-24; 40:25). Later in Zechariah's vision the
angel says to the prophet, "These seven are the eyes of the
LORD which range through the whole earth" (4:10). This is
interesting because "the eyes of the LORD" in the Old Testament refers as much to God's power as to his ability to see (2
Chron 16:9; Ps 33:13-19). We have already noted that the
Lamb in Revelation is said to have seven eyes. This tells us
there is a connection between the seven spirits and the Lamb
as well. In fact, Revelation makes precisely this point when it
describes the Lamb as having "seven eyes, which are the
seven spirits of God sent out into all the earth" (5:6).

Symbolic numbers and Old Testament images are absolutely essential for understanding the meaning of what John
saw. Once we realize that Revelation uses numbers and
images in this way, we cannot arbitrarily switch back and
forth between symbolic and literal readings of the text. That
would get us hopelessly confused, and confusion is what we
are trying to avoid.

Images, Symbols and Metaphors

Revelation's images, numbers, scenes and events all work
together to fashion an imaginary universe so compelling that
those who read the book come away changed forever. Revelation invites us to immerse ourselves in its way of depicting
reality. It wants us to suspend our experience of the world

around us for a while so that we can see, hear, smell and feel the world it is trying to depict for us. Just as when you watch a movie and for a time are caught up in the drama of the world on the screen, so Revelation uses signs, symbols and pictures to transport us to another reality.

The *Star Wars* movies are a good illustration of this. They take us to a whole new world and drop us right into the middle of an epic battle between the champions of justice and freedom on the one side and the dark empire on the other. Strange forces, grotesque creatures, high-speed space travel and terrifying weapons of mass destruction, appearing alongside more familiar human characters, combine powerfully to capture our imaginations and dazzle our senses. More than that, the extreme situations in these movies—as well as in others about alien invasions and meteorites hurtling towards the earth—allow filmmakers to explore basic human themes: What are our core values? What are we willing to die for? What is life really all about? What are the really frightening dangers facing humanity today?

One big difference between Revelation's world and the world of movies is that Revelation wants us to take its world to be even more real than the one we commonly refer to as "the real world." In fact, Revelation is out to undermine our confidence in the evidence of our own eyes. It wants us to leave behind, once and for all, the idea that what we can see with our eyes and hear with our ears is all there is. For Revelation, that is only a small part of a much bigger whole. And until we can grasp that larger whole and understand how it relates to our experience, we will not be able to understand the true nature and meaning of what we experience around us.

John's original audience continually experienced concrete expressions of Rome's overwhelming might. Rome trumpeted its own sense of invincibility every chance it got: in its buildings, its monuments, its displays of military power, even its religious ceremonies and festivals. Wherever they went, the people of the empire were always aware of Rome's ascendancy and its claims of cultural superiority. This is the vision of reality that Revelation wants to break down. It wants to destroy these images of the world and replace them with new ones—images that depict the sovereignty of the true God and reveal the sinister nature of Rome's influence.

Chapter 17 is a classic example of this kind of image replacement. Here John describes a vision of a woman who represents Rome. But she is not beautiful and elegant, befitting Rome's majesty. Instead, she is a drunken and debauched prostitute. Faced with this vile and repulsive image, John's readers are helped to see the way things really are, the ugly truth lying behind the charming facade. Rather than going along with Rome's own propaganda about itself, Revelation presents a different picture that leaves us in no doubt of what it is saying.

Revelation also draws on symbols and images that were common in the literature of that day. For instance, the depiction of the devil as a dragon and a serpent (12:9) resonates with themes that were current in Greek and Roman religion, as well as with very obvious Old Testament images. Revelation also draws from ancient folktales: in chapter 12, for example, it tells the redemption story in a way that recalls a popular ancient tale about the sun and the stars.

In a similar way Revelation heightens the sense of

impending disaster by tapping into images that evoke the average person's fears and anxieties about life. For instance, scenarios that suggest an invasion from the kings of Parthia call forth a fear similar to what westerners felt toward the Soviet Union during the Cold War. Other scenes use images of disease, volcanoes, earthquakes and environmental disasters. All these are deeply rooted in the actual events of the first century. The better we understand the particulars of that historical situation, the better we can appreciate the impact of this book on its original audience.

The Structure of Apocalyptic

Revelation's structure is not linear; it does not tell us a simple story in a straight line. At times the vision circles back and tells us the same thing it has already told us but in a different way. Also, many of the sequences of events do not simply follow one after another, but actually overlap. For example, the seven seal-openings *include* the seven trumpets, which include the seven bowls. Chapters 12–13 repeat and elaborate on things mentioned in chapter 11. Perhaps the best modern illustration of this is the way a filmmaker uses cinematic tools such as flashbacks, replays, slow motion, changes in lighting and camera angles, music, special effects and computer enhancements. Contemporary films are a highly complex medium of communication. A person who experiences his or her first movie as an adult may well find it confusing, but those of us who are familiar with this medium have little difficulty keeping pace with the twists and turns. And so it is with apocalyptic literature like the book of Revelation. Once we become familiar with the way it communicates, we will find its message much easier to follow.

At this point I can well imagine an objection—one that I myself voiced when I first began to explore this way of reading the book of Revelation. The objection is this: Didn't John simply have an amazing vision? Didn't he just write down what he saw? Why all this discussion of the literary features of a text that shouldn't be subjected to the same analysis we would use for an ordinary poem or piece of creative writing?

This objection raises an important issue indeed, which is the relationship between John's visionary experience and what he actually wrote down. Certainly we should not doubt that John did indeed have the visions he describes. But we do not have direct access to those visions. What we do have access to is a literary artifact, a carefully and thoughtfully composed account of what happened to him. And because what we have is a highly complex and profound *written* document, it is indeed entirely appropriate that we should study it using the proper literary tools. The prophetic books of the Old Testament are no different. Isaiah and Jeremiah prefaced their words with phrases like "Thus saith the Lord." Yet the rich symbolism and imagery of their compositions require us to read them *as poetry* rather than as compendiums of theology written in prose.

Conclusion

Reading Revelation requires us to have an informed imagination. We are very familiar with the idea of needing to be well informed when we read the Scriptures, but we are not so well acquainted with the idea that our knowledge should engage our imagination. We tend to associate imagination with "make believe"—things that are not true. But Revelation appeals to more than our rational sense of logic and sound argument. It appeals to our ability to picture things in our minds and our capacity to become emotionally involved with the world around us. As we read the book of Revelation we are invited to immerse ourselves in John's retelling of his visionary experience. We are called to experience something of what John experienced, and to be affected by it in the same way that he was.

But our encounter with Revelation may leave us dumbfounded if we do not keep in mind some of the principles we have discussed in this chapter. We have to listen carefully for echoes of biblical passages and keep alert for scenes and themes that relate to the first century. To hear the echoes of Old Testament language we may need to reopen our Bibles and refresh ourselves in its stories, speeches and poems. If we are not familiar with the grand themes of books like Exodus, Isaiah, Jeremiah, Zechariah and Daniel, our ears will be deaf to the subtleties of John's masterful composition, and much of the book's message will be lost to us. Similarly, if we want to hear the first-century rumblings that echo throughout the book, we need some knowledge of the basic facts of that era. Revelation is a first-century text written for first-century people. The more we know about these, the more will we be able to empathize with the author's and the first readers' fears, anxieties and hopes, and so enter into Revelation's message to them. Most of all we need to see how both the Old Testament and the situation of the first century fueled and shaped a rich and evocative world of images and symbols that combine to proclaim a powerful message about God and his claims on the world.

Finally, we need to read with a spirit of openness, to listen with our hearts as well as our minds. Many times in its opening chapters, Revelation voices the refrain, "Let anyone who has an ear listen to what the Spirit is saying to the churches." This requires us to open our own spirits to the voice of the Spirit whose message is often deeper than words or pictures or symbols. Revelation is so much more than a fantastic story about the end of time. It calls us even now to a particular kind of discipleship. It is a discipleship of following a slaughtered Lamb wherever he goes. It is a discipleship of bearing true witness to the reality of One who sits on the throne of the universe. It is also a discipleship of resistance. Revelation challenges us to stand against the powerful dragon whose imperial ambition is being played out on the world's stage. How this terrible fact intersects with our commitments, loyalties and convictions is a matter that we must work out in an attitude of listening, of openness to the Spirit, and of willingness to act on what we hear. We are called to personal participation. At the beginning of chapter 4 John sees a door standing open in heaven and he hears a voice saying, "Come up here!" Revelation invites us to join John in his experience of another world, and from there to reflect on the meaning of that experience for the life of discipleship.

As we do this we must be careful to avoid "the crystal ball syndrome"—that tendency to treat Revelation as a blueprint of the future. Revelation is indeed prophetic, but prophecy is not only about the future. The voice of the prophet calls us to hear what the Lord is saying to his people and to the world. In Revelation the prophet John cries out, "Worship God!" He teaches us how to live as people who are loyal to the One who sits on the throne and to the Lamb who was slaughtered. He instructs us about what it will take and what it will cost to resist the evil designs of the dragon. While this message does indeed relate to the future, it does not do so in a detailed predictive way. Revelation gives us "the big picture" of God's plan for the world and challenges us to live now in the light of God's claims over the universe

The message of Revelation is summed up in the terms I chose for the title of this book: the throne, the Lamb, and the dragon. This is a kind of shorthand for what Revelation is all about—but its complexity demands that we not engage in oversimplification. Related to the central themes of the throne, the Lamb and the dragon are such important matters as the difficult subject of wrath and judgment, and the book's picture of the final outcome or goal of history. Together, these give us a vision of hope for the future of humanity—a future when evil is excluded and tears are no more.

Revelation is a deeply moving book. It is crammed with some of the New Testament's most profound theology. It is one of the Bible's richest sermons. The better we understand the nature of this book and *how* it is talking to us, the better we will be able to apply its message to our own lives. But before we dive headlong into the intricacies of Revelation's message, we need to pause so we can gain some sense of how the book is put together, its overall plan. That is what the next chapter is about.

2

HOLDING IT
TOGETHER

If you have ever read a long and complex story, you know
how important it is always to keep the overall plot in mind.
Without a sense of how the story is developing as we go
along, we soon find ourselves hopelessly lost. In fact, it is
more important to know how the book develops and unfolds
as a whole than it is to be an expert on any particular isolated
bit of it.

   This certainly applies to the book of Revelation. Though not
a particularly long book, it is definitely complex. Actually,
John's vision is more like a collection of cameos or short
visionary scenes than a single sustained vision. He says, "I saw
. . ." and, "After this I saw . . ." and so on. Yet there often seems
to be no set order. The second vision may not be a sequel to
the first. In some cases it might be more like a "prequel," taking us to a point in time before the action of the first vision. Or

it might repeat or broaden or sharpen aspects of the first vision. Sometimes quite different visions simply retell the same story from a different point of view or with a new emphasis. Thus it is vital to get an overall sense of how Revelation unfolds. The sooner we do that, the better will be our understanding of the different episodes or scenes that make up the whole drama. Here, then, is that overview of Revelation; I encourage you to keep your Bible open as we progress.

At the most basic level (see table 1.1), Revelation can be divided into three sections: introduction (1:1—3:22); main vision (4:1—22:7); and conclusion (22:8-21). The brief conclusion simply wraps up the vision with warnings not to distort any of it and with a promise by Christ that he is coming very soon. Since it poses no particular problems, I will not focus any attention on it. The introduction is a little more complex; the main vision poses the biggest challenge.

Table 1.1. The Structure of Revelation

Introduction (1:1—3:22)
Main Vision (4:1—22:7)
Conclusion (22:8-21)

The Introduction

The introduction is made up of four parts (see table 1.2). The first part (1:1-3) consists of the title of the book and a blessing on all who hear and keep the words of the prophecy. The second part (1:4-8) contains a fairly standard, though somewhat expanded, letter opening in which John introduces himself and greets his readers. It also includes a hymn of praise to Christ. The third part (1:9-20) tells how the risen Christ appeared to John in a vision and instructed him to write a letter to each of seven churches in western Asia Minor. The fourth part (2:1 – 3:23) is the seven letters themselves.

Table 1.2. The Introduction

1. Title and blessing (1:1-3)
2. Greeting and hymn of praise (1:4-8)
3. Vision of Christ and introduction to the seven letters (1:9-20)
4. The letters to the seven churches (2:1 – 3:22)

Taken together, the four parts function as an important preparation for the main vision that follows. Part one establishes the ultimate source of the Revelation: it comes from God. God gave it to Jesus who gave it to an angel who gave it to John. John gave it to his readers, thus linking us by a chain of communication all the way back to God. This is John's way of asserting the divine authority of what he says; it is a word of prophecy from the throne of God. Part two gives us a clue to what Revelation is all about. It is about God. In this greeting God is described in striking trinitarian terms. John puts it this way: "Grace to you and peace from him who is and who was and who is to come, and from the seven spirits who are before his throne, and from Jesus Christ, the faithful witness, the firstborn of the dead, and the ruler of the kings of the earth" (1:4). In the last verse of the section God himself speaks: "'I am the Alpha and the Omega,' says the Lord God, who is and who was and who is to come, the Almighty" (1:8). Between these two statements about God is a joyful outburst of praise to Christ for what he has accomplished by dying for us, and an affirmation of faith in the return of Christ.

Part three begins by giving us the setting for the main vision that will begin in chapter 4. John identifies himself to his readers as "your brother who shares with you in Jesus the persecution and the kingdom and the patient endurance," and is on the island of Patmos "because of the word of God and the testimony of Jesus" (1:9). Some of John's readers were also suffering for their faith: In Pergamum, "Antipas . . . was killed amongst you" (2:13); the Smyrnaeans have endured "affliction" and "slander" (2:9); the Ephesians have been "enduring patiently" (2:3), as have the Thyatirans (2:19). John's description connects him with those readers, as well as with the ones for whom times of trouble are just around the corner (for example, 2:10). But not all John's readers have experienced persecution or opposition. Indeed, some of them seem all too comfortable in their accommodation with the world. For them John's circumstances stand as a challenge and a rebuke. John also says he was "in the spirit" (1:10), again indicating the divine origin of his experience. Part three closes with John's vision of Christ as all-powerful, the Lord of heaven and earth, the one who holds the life of the church in his hands and whose words to the churches are of absolute importance (1:12-20).

The seven letters of part four sum up the experiences, successes and failings of real-life Christian communities. Yet their struggles and triumphs represent those of all Christian communities everywhere—what is said to them is said to all who identify themselves with the person of Christ and claim loyalty to his cause. Together the letters offer both comfort and rebuke. They inspire hope as well as fear. They also provide an essential introduction to the main themes of the remainder of the book. In fact, the main vision of Revelation (chapters 4-22) simply restates and expands the message of these letters. Most of all, the letters urge us to listen up—to open our ears and hearts to what God has to say to the church. The overall impact is that, as we leave the introduction and make our way into the main vision in chapter 4, we are both chastened and expectant. We are chastened because, with the seven churches, we have been made aware of our failings; we are expectant because we have been reminded yet again of Christ's enduring love for his people. We have been made ready to receive the special message that is about to be given to us.

The Main Vision

We are now ready to face the challenge of looking at the main vision that begins in chapter 4 and runs to the middle of chapter 22. The most important thing to keep in mind here is that the whole vision, or series of visions, is centered on the very first scene that John sees. At the beginning of chapter 4 John is summoned through an open door in the sky. On passing through this door he comes face to face with a panorama of breathtaking beauty and majesty—the throne room of God (if such a place could be called a room). This initial scene is the hub of the whole book. Everything that happens after it is like spokes, radiating outward from this vision of God on his throne, the seven spirits who are before the throne, and the Lamb that was slaughtered. Chapter 4 sets up the primary truth that Revelation impresses on us: God is seated on his throne and is surrounded by the perpetual worship of the hosts of heaven. Chapter 5 then sets in motion the drama that will take us through the rest of the vision: the One on the throne holds a sealed scroll that only the Lamb is able to open. The opening of the scroll in chapter 6 is the beginning of the rest of the vision.

What I have said so far shows that Revelation can be divided into a number of different levels. The throne scene is on level one. What follows is on level two because it flows from what happens on level one. Further into the book we find several passages that are on level three because they elaborate or expand on things that happen on level two. Table 1.3 divides the main vision into these three levels.

The three levels provide a quick overview of the content of the book. As the table shows, only two scenes occur at level one: the initial throne scene and the picture of the new heaven and earth at the very end. This tells us the vision's direction. It opens with a picture of God's rule in heaven and ends with a picture of God's rule spanning the universe—God's kingdom has come to earth. Level two includes events associated with the three series of judgments: the seals, the trumpets, and the bowls. These prepare for the coming of God's kingdom by purging the earth of sin and godlessness. Level three consists of scenes that tell us more about the events on level two, taking us deeper and revealing new mysteries.

Level two begins with the seven seals that keep the scroll shut. These are no ordinary seals; as each one is broken it unleashes an event or series of events that lead up to the unrolling of the scroll itself. All the seals must be broken before the scroll can be read, so the breaking of the seals continually heightens our anticipation and expectation for what

Table 1.3

Level 1	Level 2	Level 3
The throne scene (4—5)		
	The seal-openings (6:1—8:5), including first pause (7)	
	The trumpet blasts (8:6—11:19), including second pause (10:1—11:14)	
		The woman and the dragon (12)
		The two beasts (13)
		The Lamb and the 144,000 (14:1-5)
		The three angels (14:6-13)
		The two harvests (14:14-20)
	The plague bowls (15—16)	
		The great prostitute (17)
		The fall of Babylon (18)
		Rejoicing in heaven (19:1-10)
		The rider on the white horse (19:11-21)
		The millennium (20:1-10)
		Final judgment (20:11-15)
The new cosmos (21—22:7)		

is in the scroll itself. As if this delay were not enough, John's vision takes a number of detours. Just when we think we can hardly bear the tension any longer we are sidetracked to a different scene. Thus, right after the sixth seal has been broken,

when we think we are finally going to witness the breaking of
the last seal, an extended detour takes the whole of chapter 7.
Only at the beginning of chapter 8 do we come at last to the
seventh seal-opening. Even then there are more delays in
store for us because the breaking of the seventh seal sets in
motion not just a single event but seven more events: the
seven trumpet blasts. Then the whole sequence is repeated:
six trumpets blasts, another detour, then the seventh blast.

The detours or pauses are not just teasers. They have an
important message, if we are patient enough to listen. Both of
them tell us crucial things about what it means to be followers of the Lamb, and what our own role is in the working out
of God's amazing purposes. We will return later to these
important passages.

The seventh trumpet blast is indeed a momentous event.
After it has sounded, loud voices in heaven declare: "The
kingdom of the world has become the kingdom of our Lord
and of his Messiah, and he will reign forever and ever"
(11:15). Then the twenty-four elders, who are part of the
throne room of God, sing: "We give you thanks, Lord God
Almighty, who are and who were, for you have taken your
great power and begun to reign" (11:17).

This ushering in of the kingdom of God is the fulfillment
of the first petition of the Lord's Prayer: "Thy kingdom come,
Thy will be done on earth as it is in heaven." We feel that we
have arrived. But John's vision is not even half over. Eleven
more chapters are yet to come. Nevertheless, this is a good
time to pause and take stock of how far we have advanced.
The scroll that was in the hand of God has been opened. In
the process all seven seals have been broken and all seven

trumpets sounded—God's kingdom has arrived! In addition, there have been two pauses: one between the opening of the sixth and seventh seal; the other between the blasting of the sixth and seventh trumpet. The broad strokes of the vision have been painted; all the rest is expansion and elaboration of this basic material.

Chapters 12-14 go into detail about the conflict that God's people are a part of. Chapter 12 talks about a war with a terrifying seven-headed dragon; chapter 13 adds two more monsters, one from the sea and one from the land. These are the dragon's henchmen who do his dirty work for him. The first part of chapter 14 depicts the followers of the Lamb as a company of martyrs who "follow the Lamb wherever he goes" (14:4). These are all matters we will return to later.

From 14:6 onward, the focus shifts to final judgment and the destruction of the forces of evil. First, three angels announce messages of warning to the inhabitants of the earth (14:6-13). Next, John sees a vision of two harvests, one of grain and one of grapes, which stand for the gathering in of the Lamb's followers to himself and of the beast's followers to destruction. This is followed in chapters 15 and 16 by another series of momentous events in which seven plague bowls, full of the wrath of God, are poured out on the earth. These bowls are closely related to the seventh trumpet, just as the trumpets were closely related to the seventh seal-opening: The seventh seal-opening unleashed the seven trumpets, and the seventh trumpet unleashes the seven plague bowls. As we shall see later, one effect of this sequence is to focus our attention on the final events of each series. It also clearly indicates an increased intensity: the events associated with the trumpet blasts are more severe than those associated with the seals, and the plague bowls are worse yet. In fact, the series of plague bowls has no pause between the sixth and seventh pouring. By this point in the vision events are moving at break-neck speed to the inevitable conclusion. There is no more time for delay.

This takes us to the end of chapter 16. Chapters 17-19 are elaborations and expansions of aspects of the sixth and seventh plague bowls. They include the destruction of the great prostitute (who stands for Rome), the fall of Babylon (which also stands for Rome) and the final battle between the dragon's monsters and the rider on the white horse (Christ). Next comes chapter 20, which speaks of a thousand-year reign of Christ on earth. A brief rebellion and the final destruction of the dragon follow this. Then comes the final judgment, as all the inhabitants of the earth stand before the great throne of God to account for their lives. In chapters 21-22, John sees a vision of a new heaven and a new earth from which evil and suffering are excluded and in which God himself dwells among his people. The vision ends with the words of Jesus: "See, I am coming soon! Blessed is the one who keeps the words of the prophecy of this book" (22:7).

In conclusion, I want to emphasize once again that Revelation does not unfold in a straightforward sequential way. Many times the action of the visions takes us back over territory we have already covered, introducing new information, changed perspectives and surprising twists of plot. We have to be constantly aware of where we are in the development of the book; the outline and overview in this chapter should be of some assistance.

3

THE THRONE

The central image of Revelation is in chapter 4, the scene that meets John's eyes when he passes through the heavenly door: God seated on a great throne and surrounded by perpetual worship. This is the core reality, more real than everything else we know. Next to it, all other things become strangely unreal. They lose their substance and become shadowy. Revelation is a book about realizing this fact and bringing our lives into line with it. A life focused on God is founded on a solid foundation. A life focused on anything else is founded on a mist, a vapor, a lie.

Much later in Revelation, as his vision nears its end, John is so overwhelmed by all he has seen that twice he falls down to worship his angelic guide. Both times he is roundly rebuked and told in no uncertain terms to "worship God" (19:10; 22:11). And that is the fundamental message of Revelation: Worship God! We need to reflect carefully on what it means.

The One on the Throne

The throne of God is mentioned many times in Revelation, and its basic meaning is easily understood. It tells us that God is sovereign, that he is the ultimate authority over the entire universe. Modern secular humanity immediately balks at this. It is one thing to be impressed by the beauty and grandeur of the throne, but it is quite another to welcome what the throne stands for. Those of us who have grown up in liberal democratic societies often react negatively to the idea of absolute, unquestioned authority. Yet we cannot escape the fact that God is presented in Revelation as a monarch or emperor, an idea that John's original audience would have found much more natural and self-evident than we do. God is awesome and beautiful to behold, *and* he is the ruler of the world. Indeed, one of Revelation's favorite ways of talking about God is simply to refer to him as the "one seated on the throne."

This, of course, is not a new idea. Already among the Hebrew prophets we find many references to God on a throne. In 1 Kings 22:19, for example, the prophet Micaiah states, "I saw the LORD sitting on his throne, with all the host of heaven standing beside him to the right and to the left of him." Longer descriptions of similar scenes are given in Isaiah 6:1-3, Ezekiel 1:4-28 and Daniel 7:9-10. They all depict God seated on a throne surrounded by heavenly beings, and in each case they challenge human pretensions to power.

Civilizations, empires and superpowers have always tried

to achieve invincibility and to set themselves up as divine in some sense. These biblical visions remind us that only God is truly supreme. Therefore, God alone has the right to be worshiped. Revelation develops this theme in a number of ways, including emphasizing the mystery and beauty of God on the throne. John begins his account of his vision by telling us that he saw on the throne someone who "looks like jasper and carnelian" (4:3). These are reddish-yellow varieties of quartz that, in this context, give us a sense of the beauty, luminosity and wonder of what John saw. Their solidity might also suggest stability or permanence. Of course, John is not giving us a physical description of God. Like the Old Testament prophets before him, he uses expressions that tell us he is unable to give a clear picture of what he saw. In this case he uses the phrase "looks like" to indicate that his description is at best an approximation of his experience.

Next, he tells us that "around the throne is a rainbow that looks like an emerald" (4:3). The rainbow is a reminder of God's covenant with Noah, and thus a reminder of God's faithfulness and mercy. In a book that has much to say about judgment and wrath, we are first assured of God's unfailing love and promise to the people of the earth. But this is no ordinary rainbow. John says it looks like an emerald, again deepening our sense of the beauty and mystery and permanence of God's throne. A natural rainbow is a mirage, a temporary visual effect caused by the refraction of light through water vapor. The emerald rainbow and what it stands for is much more real than that.

Thunder and Lightning

John also tells us that from the throne came flashes of lightning, and rumblings and peals of thunder (4:5). These details are reminders, or echoes, of that very important Old Testament scene at Mount Sinai:

> On the morning of the third day there was thunder and lightning as well as a thick cloud on the mountain, and a blast of a trumpet so loud that all the people who were in the camp trembled. . . . Now Mount Sinai was wrapped in smoke, because the LORD had descended upon it in fire; the smoke went up like the smoke of a kiln, while the whole mountain shook violently. And as the blast of the trumpet grew louder and louder, Moses would speak and God would answer him in thunder. . . . When all the people witnessed the thunder and lightning, the sound of the trumpet and the mountain smoking, they were afraid and trembled and stood at a distance. (Ex 19:16-19; 20:18)

This scene depicts God's majesty and the awe that it rightly inspires. Its parallel in the book of Revelation reminds us of God's law because of the association with Mount Sinai. Together they tell us of God's holiness, as do the living creatures with their cry, "Holy, holy, holy."

The Crystal Sea

John's description of the throne of God also includes a reference to "something like a sea of glass, like crystal" in front of the throne (4:6). The sea is a rich and complex symbol in Revelation. In fact, there is more than one sea, so we must distinguish between them. The sea that John saw before God's throne is a heavenly one, first hinted at in the Genesis creation account. There we are told that on the second day God said, "Let there be a dome in the midst of the waters, and let it separate the waters from the waters" (Gen 1:6). God separates "the waters" into two parts: the waters above the dome (or sky), and the waters beneath the dome. The waters beneath are what we know as the sea; the waters above are a kind of heavenly sea. This heavenly sea is what John encounters before the throne.

The sea beneath the sky, our earthly sea, becomes very important later on in Revelation. Ancient writers often treated it as a symbol of the abyss: the home of evil and the dwelling place of monsters. The Canaanites, for example, believed a terrifying monster called Leviathan inhabited the sea. (Interestingly, Leviathan had seven heads, just like the dragon in Revelation.) The Babylonians had a myth in which one of their gods, called Marduk, fought and defeated Tiamat, the monstrous goddess of chaos who lived in the sea. When the battle was over, Marduk cut Tiamat's body in two and made the heavens out of one half and earth out of the other. The monster from the deep had to be destroyed before creation could take place.

In a similar way, several Old Testament writers used the idea of a great battle between God and a terrible sea monster when they wanted to speak of God's rule and sovereignty over creation. A classic example is where the psalmist says to the Lord: "You divided the sea by your might; you broke the heads of the dragons in the waters. You crushed the heads of Leviathan; you gave him as food for the creatures of the wilderness" (Ps 74:13-14). And the prophet Isaiah wrote, "On that day the LORD with his cruel and great and strong sword will

punish Leviathan the fleeing serpent, Leviathan the twisting
serpent, and he will kill the dragon that is in the sea" (Is 27:1).

In other places the sea itself is a hostile force that has to be
conquered and brought under control. God asks Job: "Who
shut in the sea with doors when it burst from the womb?—
when I made the clouds its garment, and thick darkness its
swaddling band, and prescribed bounds for it, and set bars
and doors, and said, 'Thus far you shall come and no farther,
and here shall your proud waves be stopped'?" (Job 38:8-11).
And the psalmist declares, "At your rebuke [the waters] flee;
at the sound of your thunder they take to flight. They rose up
to the mountains, ran down to the valleys to the place that
you appointed for them. You set a boundary that they may
not pass, so that they might not again cover the earth" (Ps
104:5-9).

These writers used the sea as a symbol of chaotic and evil
forces, clamoring to swallow up God's created order. The
earthly sea in Revelation has the same symbolic value. Thus,
the terrible beast of chapter 13 comes up *from the sea* (as did
the four monsters of Dan 7). And it is significant that when
John speaks about the new heaven and the new earth at the
end of Revelation, the first thing he has to say is that "the sea
was no more" (21:1). But the heavenly sea in the throne
scene of chapter 4 is not a chaotic or hostile force. It is completely calm, transparent and beautiful—uncontaminated by
the forces of darkness and chaos in the world. It tells us what
yet will be when God's kingdom is established on earth.

The Twenty-Four Elders

As with almost everything in Revelation, the identity and

function of the group of twenty-four elders has been the subject of much speculation by scholars. Some think they correspond to the twenty-four bodyguards who stood around the emperor Domitian and symbolized his imperial authority. Perhaps a better interpretation draws on the fact that in Judaism at that time the temple priesthood was divided into twenty-four "courses" or "shifts." Keeping in mind that Revelation considers all God's people to be priests, the twenty-four elders may be the heavenly representatives of God's priestly people. That each of them has a golden incense bowl full of the prayers of the saints (5:8) clearly indicates their priestly role. They are also rulers because they wear crowns and sit on thrones. This fits in with the way Revelation speaks of Christians as a kingdom of priests (20:6; compare Ex 19:6).

Like others in the scene, the twenty-four elders worship God. Abandoning their thrones and laying down their crowns at his feet, they prostrate themselves in humility before the great and glorious One. By their reverential homage they signify their place under God's ultimate rule. Their thrones are not rivals to God's. In no way do they detract from the glory that is ascribed to God in this scene.

The Living Creatures

The four living creatures seem similar to the "seraphs" of Isaiah's vision (Is 6:2) and Ezekiel's "living creatures" (Ezek 1:4-21). These two prophetic visions parallel the angelic beings that were part of the ark of the covenant (called "cherubim," plural for "cherub," but quite unlike the flying babies of popular imagination—see 1 Sam 4:4; 2 Sam 6:2; Ps 80:1; 99:10).

The ark itself represented God's throne and the cherubim were understood to be standing in attendance upon him. Interestingly, descriptions of these angelic beings are never quite the same from one passage to the next. For example, Revelation's four living creatures each have one face, while the four creatures in Ezekiel each have four faces. Revelation's creatures each have six wings as in Isaiah, not four as in Ezekiel. In Revelation they are full of eyes; in Ezekiel the eyes are on the rims of the wheels of God's throne. What these discrepancies (if that is what we should call them) underscore is the difficulty the prophets had in describing what they experienced. More to the point, they show us that these prophets, divinely inspired as they were, crafted what they saw so it would communicate something specific to us. As I emphasized earlier, Revelation is not John's vision, it is the literary distillation of John's vision. Thus it uses literary techniques that must to be taken into account if we are to understand John's message.

Having said that, it is likely the four living creatures of Revelation represent the whole created cosmos of heaven and earth. Their role is to spend their whole lives worshiping God. They are a kind of object lesson of the core message of Revelation. Together with the twenty-four elders they demonstrate all creation's appropriate response to God. "Day and night without ceasing they sing, 'Holy, holy, holy, the Lord God the Almighty who was and is and is to come'" (4:8; compare Is 6:2-3). More than that, they drive home the key point that Revelation is trying to make: at the very heart of reality is the worship of the One who sits on the throne. Our ultimate destiny as creatures will be determined by the extent to which we either resonate with or rebel against this reality.

Words About God

The portrayal of God in the throne scene is supplemented by the distinctive ways Revelation refers to God: "'I am the Alpha and the Omega,' says the Lord God, who is and who was and who is to come, the Almighty" (1:8). This verse includes three of Revelation's main ways of talking about God: the Alpha and the Omega; the One who is and was and is to come; the Lord God, the Almighty. It has added significance in being one of just two places in the book where we hear God actually speaking. And in the second place, God also says "I am the Alpha and the Omega," adding "the beginning and the end" (21:6). Since God uses these titles to identify himself, we need to consider them closely.

The Alpha and the Omega. Alpha and omega are the first and last letters of the Greek alphabet. Their use here as meaning something like, "I am the first one and the last one" is confirmed by the addition of "the beginning and the end" (21:6). So far so good, but what does it mean?

Both the term for "beginning" *(arche)* and the term for "end" *(telos)* are packed with significance. "Beginning" can mean "source," as a spring might be the beginning of a river. In this sense the word points toward God the Creator, the one from whom all things originate and by whom they continue to exist. Thus, the title speaks of the dependence of everything on God. As John's Gospel puts it, speaking of the Word: "All things came into being through him, and without him not one thing came into being" (Jn 1:3). In Revelation the heavenly chorus gives glory to God precisely because "you created all things, and by your will they existed and were created" (4:11). The word *arche* can also mean "ruler," so that God is not just the Creator on whom all life depends, but also the one who oversees all life and to whom all living things are ultimately responsible.

The description of God as the "end" speaks to us of the goal or purpose of the world. A river's end is the sea—that is its destination; that is where it finishes. But "end" also means "outcome" or "purpose," the reason why we do something. God is both the destination of creation and its purpose, its point. At the close of time, at the completion of all human activity, there stands the throne of God. Life comes from God and it returns to God. Thus all of life is encompassed by God (see Acts 17:28), a thought that should shape how we live in the world day by day.

The phrase "the first and the last" also echoes what Yahweh announces in Isaiah: "I am the first and I am the last; besides me there is no God. Who is like me? Let them proclaim it. . . . There is no other rock; I know not one" (Is 44:6-8). Here it emphasizes that God is the *only* one, the be-all-and-end-all of everything. No one—and especially not the manufactured gods of human ingenuity—can rival God's supremacy.

Revelation does not distinguish between God and Jesus when it comes to the title "Alpha and Omega, beginning and end." In Revelation 22:13 it is Jesus who states, "I am the Alpha and the Omega, the first and the last, the beginning and the end," and in 1:17 Jesus refers to himself as the "first and the last." This is part of Revelation's very clear message about the deity of Christ, which we will return to a little later.

The One who is and who was and who is to come. This expression occurs three times in its full form (1:4, 8; 4:8) and twice in an abbreviated form, "he who is and who was" (11:17; 16:5). It is apparently an explanation of the name of God given to Moses in Exodus 3:14, where God identified himself as "I AM," and "I AM WHO I AM" (or "I will be who I will be"). Ancient Jewish and Christian interpreters of the Bible took these words to be declarations of God's timelessness, the fact that God is always there, was always there, and will always be there. The scholars who translated the Hebrew Scriptures into Greek in the centuries before the birth of Christ used the expression "the being one" to capture this sense of God being the one who always is, who is always present.

John's expression in Revelation has a similar meaning but is distinct because of the last phrase: "and *who is coming.*" He thus emphasizes not just God's eternity but also the fact that God is about to arrive. The two abbreviated versions omit this ending because by that stage in the vision God has already arrived. As the twenty-four elders proclaim, "We give you thanks, Lord God Almighty, who are and who were, *for you have taken your great power and begun to reign*" (11:17). God is no longer the one who will arrive—he has now come in all his power.

The Lord God the Almighty. This title appears in Revelation seven times (1:8; 4:8; 11:17; 15:3; 16:7; 19:6; 21:22), which reminds us of the special care that John took in composing his account of the vision. Once again this is a title that has strong links to the Old Testament (for example, 2 Sam 5:10;

Jer 5:14) where it points to God's supremacy over the universe in general and his control over the unfolding of history in particular. In Revelation its sevenfold recurrence drives home the central message that the One on the throne—not the one in Rome, not the dragon, not anything else—is in control of the course of history. The emperor Domitian, remember, wanted people to call him "Lord and God." Revelation's point is at once a message of comfort to John's Christian readers and a word of challenge to the powers of the world. Though the world may seem to be under the control of forces other than God, this is a temporary state of affairs. There is a time coming, and it is coming soon, when the entire world will see and acknowledge that it is the Lord God who is the Almighty One.

The three titles together form a coherent and powerful picture of the central character of the book of Revelation. They are, of course, only part of the way Revelation depicts God. Many other references point to other aspects of his nature and his activity in the world. Most important for us, though, is the way Revelation urges us to relate to God in worship. At the end of chapter 4, the entire scene culminates in a crescendo of praise and worship:

> And whenever the living creatures give glory and honor and thanks to the one who is seated on the throne, who lives forever and ever, the twenty-four elders fall before the one who is seated on the throne and worship the one who lives forever and ever; they cast their crowns before the throne saying, "You are worthy, our Lord and God, to receive glory and honor and power, for you created all things, and by your will they existed and were created." (4:9-11)

Worship is the appropriate response to God: whole-hearted, awe-inspired, loving worship. In fact, Revelation implies it is the only authentic response. For in worship we rightly acknowledge the awesomeness of God and our total dependence on him. But worship is expressed in more than just songs or prayers; it is expressed in loyalty. Revelation speaks of a great battle between the One who sits on the throne and the dragon who aspires to that position himself. Revelation calls us to think deeply about what it means to be loyal to the One on the throne, even though the world seems dead-set against believing that he even exists. It challenges us to count the cost of being associated with God and his ways of working in the world—and the consequences of not being associated with God's great purposes for the history of the world.

The Worship of God

In the next two chapters I will spell out some of the implications of being a worshiper of God. As we will see, worshiping God is both practical and all-embracing. The apostle Paul likened it to utter and complete self-sacrifice. Writing to the Christians at the heart of the Roman Empire, he said, "I appeal to you therefore, brothers and sisters, by the mercies of God, to present your bodies as a living sacrifice, holy and acceptable to God, which is your spiritual worship" (Rom 12:1). Paul's metaphor spoke powerfully and materially to the way Christ's followers live in a world that is often hostile to faith and opposed to God. He saw his own life as an act of sacrifice, a pouring out of everything he had and was in the service of God and his people (see Phil 2:17; 2 Tim 4:6). To worship God meant toil, it meant putting others ahead of himself. Ultimately it meant following the example of Jesus (see 2 Cor 8:9; Phil 2:5-8). This is the message of Revelation as well. To worship God means to follow the Lamb; it means to give allegiance to him in the great battle with the dragon. These are practical lessons that we will focus on in more detail in the next two chapters.

Finally we should notice that in Revelation, to worship God is also to worship Christ. The picture of the Lamb, which we will look at more closely in the next chapter, reveals God's very essence and nature. The figure on the throne shows us one aspect of who God is; the Lamb shows us another—and neither is less important. Thus John reports, "Then I heard every creature in heaven and on earth and under the earth and in the sea, and all that is in them singing, 'To the one seated on the throne *and to the Lamb* be blessing and honor and glory and might forever and ever!'" (5:13).

When the book draws to a close with the vision of the New Jerusalem, the One on the throne and the Lamb are still intimately linked. The river of life flows "from the throne of God and of the Lamb" (22:1). A little later we read, "Nothing accursed will be found there anymore. But the throne of God and of the Lamb will be in it, and *his* servants will worship *him*. They will see *his* face and *his* name will be on their foreheads" (22:3-4). Technically correct grammar would lead us to expect the last phrases to say, "and *their* servants will worship *them*" and so on. But Revelation wants us to see very clearly the intimate relationship—the oneness—between the One on the throne and the Lamb. Earlier, it said of "the holy ones": "they will be priests of God and of Christ, and they will

reign with *him* a thousand years" (20:6). Thus Revelation proclaims that Christ is not just a special agent sent to do God's
will, nor is he even an angelic figure (recall that Revelation
rejects worshiping angels). Rather, he is God who shares with
the One on the throne the worship of the entire created
order. Just what it means to follow this Christ is what we
must look at next.

4

THE LAMB

We have already seen that God is the central character of Revelation; to worship God is to acknowledge his awesomeness and our utter dependence on him. But more than that, to worship God means to follow the Lamb. This is what we will explore now.

The Scroll and the Lamb

Chapter 5 introduces something new into the scene of worship: the One sitting on the throne is holding a scroll affixed with seven seals. What is in the scroll? Why is it sealed? Will it be opened? These questions, which rightly intrigue us, also cause us a sense of alarm because of John's deeply emotional response to the news that no one is worthy to open the scroll. At this point we are forced to play "catch up" because John is obviously much more aware than we are of the significance of what is going on in this scene. He knows that the scroll contains something highly significant. But as long as it remains shut, its contents will remain inaccessible and useless—shelved forever. John's despair and frustration overflow in bitter tears at the very thought of it.

The dilemma in this scene has an intriguing parallel in a well-known legend: the story from King Arthur's day of the sword embedded in the stone. As that ancient story goes, the sorcerer Merlin devised a test that would identify the true heir to the throne. Only the individual who could dislodge a magical sword embedded in rock would have the right to rule. Arthur pulls the sword from the stone, making clear to everyone that he is the rightful king.

A similar scenario is played out in Revelation, only here the task is to open the sealed scroll. This calls for someone with particular qualifications; he must be the true heir. At first the right person is nowhere to be found: "And no one in heaven or on earth or under the earth was able to open the scroll or to look into it" (5:2-3). At this point John is overwhelmed by a sense of doom—the tension of the moment is palpable. But profound relief is at hand: "Then one of the elders said to me, 'Do not weep. See, the Lion of the tribe of Judah, the Root of David, has conquered, so that he can open the scroll and its seven seals'"(5:5).

Someone *is* worthy to open the scroll! All is not lost. The sword in the stone will be dislodged. Having learned this, though, our sense of relief must not cause us to miss some of the vital detail of what is going on right before our eyes. What we are looking at here contains one of the keys to solving the entire riddle of John's vision. Notice the ways in which

Christ is described in this verse: first as *the Lion of the tribe of Judah*, then as *the Root of David*. Both these titles evoke long-standing messianic hopes. Both get at the essence of what the people of God expected in a savior. He would be like a lion rising to devour its prey, and he would reinvigorate the long defunct royal line of David, ancient Israel's greatest son.

By using these titles for Jesus, the elder declares that he is indeed the long-awaited Messiah. However, Revelation does not leave it at that. Rather, John's next experience results in a radical reinterpretation of these expectations, turning them upside down. The celestial elder tells John that someone has been found worthy to open the scroll. That is what John *hears*. But when John looks, what he actually *sees* is "a Lamb standing as if it had been slaughtered" (5:6). John would have expected to see a royal military figure ready for battle. What he actually saw must have been deeply perplexing—a vision of weakness rather than of strength.

The figure of a slaughtered lamb takes us back to the first Passover, when a lamb was butchered in each household to rescue the Israelites from slavery in Egypt. The lamb's blood, smeared on the doorposts and lintels of the houses of the Israelites, protected them from the angel of death as it passed through the land, killing the firstborn son of every family (Ex 12:21-23). In later times the slaughtered lamb came to be thought of as a kind of ransom that had been paid for the people's release from slavery to an overwhelming power (for example, Deut 7:8; 13:5). And this is the way the first followers of Jesus came to think of his death on the cross. He had become the ransom paid to rescue God's people from the evil kingdom. His death on the cross, followed by his resurrection from the dead, proved that he was God's anointed one, the Messiah, the true heir.

That is why he is worthy to open the scroll. Revelation puts it this way: "You are worthy to take the scroll and to open its seals, for you were slaughtered and by your blood you ransomed for God saints from every tribe and language and people and nation; you have made them to be a kingdom and priests serving our God, and they will reign on earth" (5:9-10). The last part of that passage echoes the words spoken by God to the Israelites when they eventually arrived at Mount Sinai after escaping from Egypt: "Now therefore, if you obey my voice and keep my covenant, you shall be my treasured possession out of all the peoples. Indeed the whole earth is mine, but you shall be for me a priestly kingdom and a holy nation" (Ex 19:5-6). Jesus' death is the event that brings us to God and makes it possible for us to belong to God as a treasured possession.

Another Old Testament source also helps us understand the meaning of the slaughtered Lamb in Revelation. In the book of Isaiah we find references to the exodus not as a past historical event, but as something that is still being hoped for in the future, as if another dramatic rescue of God's people is still to come. The prophet foretold a time when God's people would once again be rescued from their troubles, as they had been in the time of their Egyptian slavery: "And the *ransomed* of the Lord shall return and come to Zion with singing; everlasting joy shall be on their heads; they shall obtain joy and gladness, and sorrow and sighing shall flee away" (Is 35:10; see also 51:11).

It is as if Isaiah envisaged another exodus, after which

God's jubilant people would finally enter the Promised Land—or more precisely, Zion, the beautiful city of God. Later in Isaiah we learn that the redemption or rescue of God's people is connected to a slaughtered lamb, though this time not a literal one. It is the Lord's suffering servant, of whom it is said, "He was oppressed, and he was afflicted, yet he did not open his mouth; *like a lamb that is led to the slaughter,* and like a sheep that before its shearers is silent, so he did not open his mouth" (Is 53:7). By portraying Jesus as a slaughtered Lamb, Revelation wants us to see that he is the one who makes possible the final exodus, the ultimate rescue of God's people from sin and the forces of evil, so that they can enter rejoicing into the heavenly city.

This "new exodus" theme is scattered throughout the book of Revelation and forms one of the vision's main messages. Many of the plagues that God pours out on the earth in Revelation remind us of the plagues of Egypt at the time of the exodus: water turning to blood, hail and locusts, to name a few. In Revelation, the woman being carried on the wings of a great eagle (12:14) is an echo of God's words to the Israelites: "You have seen what I did to the Egyptians, and how I bore you on eagles' wings and brought you to myself" (Ex 19:4). Revelation 2:14 refers to Balaam and Balak, characters featured in the wilderness wanderings of the Israelites (see Num 22–23). Revelation 15:2-4 depicts the followers of the Lamb praising God in the same way that the Israelites did after God brought them safely through the Red Sea (Ex 15:1-21).

In these ways and many others, Revelation tells us to think of the life of faith as a kind of replaying of the Old Testament wilderness wanderings of God's people. A significant event has happened to rescue us from the domain of the evil one. This event is the death of the Lamb—Jesus' death on the cross. But we have yet to reach our final destination. We are still on the way. Our present experience is of the trials and hardships of the desert.

There is yet another dimension to the meaning of the slaughtered Lamb. It tells us something about how God goes about his work in the world. Unlike earthly superpowers that get their way by brute force or manipulation, God achieves his purposes through the apparent weakness and defeat of a sacrificial victim. As we ponder this amazing truth, we are faced with the same lesson the apostle Paul had to learn when he pleaded with God to remove his "thorn in the flesh." Rather than being miraculously healed, he was told, "My grace is sufficient for you, for power is made perfect in weakness" (2 Cor 12:9). God gave Paul weakness so that he would learn to rely on God's strength. What looks weak to us is powerful in God's hand, and what looks strong to us is puny in God's sight. As Paul put it in another place, "God's weakness is stronger than human strength. . . . God chose what is weak in the world to shame the strong" (1 Cor 1:25, 27).

The slaughtered Lamb is God's way of showing contempt for the power of the world. When God determines to establish his kingdom, he doesn't do it as the Romans did, with invading armies and intimidation. Rather, he does it through the humiliating death of Jesus. This has far-reaching implications for those of us who claim to follow Christ. He is a slaughtered Lamb. If we want to follow him, we should not expect our experience in the world to be much different from his. In fact, as we shall see in the next section, those who follow the way of the slaughtered Lamb will, in many respects, live a life like his.

The Followers of the Lamb

Chapter 5 leads us to expect something momentous from the sealed scroll. Those expectations are quickly fulfilled as the scroll begins to be opened, setting in motion three series of judgments that are poured out on the earth to prepare for the final establishment of God's reign. After the seal-openings come the seven trumpet blasts, bringing with them more judgments. Then the seven bowls of judgment are poured out on the earth. Each successive series is more intense than the one before; they portray God's unremitting anger on a sinful world.

However, built into the first two series of judgments are (as we have seen) two passages that substantially break the sequence, introducing a pause in the outpouring of the judgments. These passages contain vital information relating to the overall message of the book of Revelation, and particularly to those who identify themselves with the Lamb. The first of them comes in chapter 7, where we are introduced to the followers of the Lamb. The second comes in chapters 10 and 11.

The 144,000. Chapter 7 starts with four angels "holding back the winds of the earth so that no wind could blow on earth or sea or against any tree" (7:1). It becomes clear in the opening paragraph that these are destructive winds. More than that, they are equivalent to the four horsemen of the first four seal-openings. This interpretation is suggested by the book of Zechariah, which also has four horses, or chariots, that are simultaneously identified with the four winds of the earth (Zech 6:2-5). Thus this passage takes us back to a point when the four horsemen of chapter 6 were still being restrained. The reason for this restraint is so that the servants of God can be marked on their foreheads with a seal (7:3-4).

This mark or seal is a sign of ownership. It shows that these people belong to God, distinguishing them from those who do not. When we encounter them again, we are told that the mark on their foreheads is nothing less than the name of the Lamb and of his Father (14:1). The same point is made again in 22:4. Earlier we learned that the mark is a source of protection because the locusts from the bottomless pit are told to harm "only those who *do not* have the seal of God on their foreheads" (9:4). This should not lead us to think that Revelation promises a life free of suffering for the people of the Lamb. In fact the opposite is the truth, as we shall see. But the main point here is that Christ has put his mark or seal on those who belong to him. It is a spiritual badge or nametag. The apostle Paul used a similar concept when he wrote of people being marked with the seal of the Holy Spirit (Eph 1:13-14).

John next tells us that he "heard the number of those who were sealed, one hundred forty-four thousand" (7:4). Here we must be sensitive to how John is using numbers and biblical imagery if we are going to get the point of what he is telling us. The number 144,000—twelve thousand from each of the twelve tribes of Israel (7:5-8)—is highly charged with symbolic significance. It does not represent a literal group of this exact number, but stands for the entire people of God. In 5:5-6 we noticed a contrast between what John heard and what he saw. Here again, John *heard* the number 144,000 (7:4), but when he looked what he actually *saw* was "a great multitude that no one can count, from every nation, from all tribes and peoples and languages" (7:9).

Notice how John's vision specifically addresses two important issues: the number of people and their origins. The number was countless, and they came from absolutely everywhere. John is not telling us that he saw two groups, one of 144,000 Israelites and another of innumerable Gentiles. Both descriptions refer to the same group of people. The 144,000 *is* the innumerable multitude, and vice versa—the same way that the Lion of Judah is the Lamb who was slaughtered, and the Lamb is the Lion of Judah. Revelation presents its readers with a radical reinterpretation of traditional expectations. The final tally of God's people will include individuals from every corner of the globe, not just people from ethnic Israel. Indeed, the great multitude from many nations may be understood as a fulfillment of God's promise to the patriarch Abraham. God assured Abraham that through him all the nations of the earth would be blessed, and that his descendants would be as the sand of the sea and the stars of the heavens (Gen 13:16; 15:5; 32:12). This is exactly what Revelation depicts.

The difference between the 144,000 and the great multitude is not just a matter of size and ethnicity. They also have contrasting functions. The 144,000 are soldiers. We know this by the way that they are counted out—twelve thousand from each of the twelve tribes. It is the roll call of a mighty force, the army of the Lion of Judah, an echo of the military census of the Israelites in the wilderness (Num 1:1-3). By contrast, the great multitude is a company of martyrs. These are the people of the slaughtered Lamb. Listen to the conversation that takes place between John and one of the heavenly elders:

> Then one of the elders addressed me saying, "Who are these robed in white, and where have they come from?" I said to him, "Sir, you are the one that knows." Then he said to me, "These are they who have come out of the great ordeal; they have washed their robes and made them white in the blood of the Lamb." (7:13-14)

This brief exchange is vital for understanding what Revelation is saying to us about the people of the Lamb. Two aspects of the elder's words are particularly important: his reference to "the great ordeal," and his reference to robes washed in the blood of the Lamb. I will begin with the second, then return to the first.

The most significant thing to notice about the washed robes is that they are washed by the ones who wear them. This is striking because we might have expected the elder to say that their robes were washed by the Lamb—that is, that their sins had been forgiven because of the blood Jesus shed on their behalf. Instead, the image is one of *active involvement*. The multitudes robed in white deliberately aligned themselves with the Lamb who was slaughtered. They chose to be linked with him by dipping their clothes in his blood. What does this mean? Simply that they have identified themselves with him completely. They stand for what he stands for. They continue his message in the world. And because of that, they share his experience of the world, even to the point where they "follow the Lamb wherever he goes" (14:4).

Ultimately this means they have shared in his death by their own deaths. They are martyrs just as he was a martyr.

The Greek word for "martyr" *(martys)* basically means "witness," a person who tells what they know or have seen (with dying being the most radical form of witnessing). Revelation calls Jesus himself the faithful and true witness, and those who follow him continue his message. For him, being a witness was all about proclaiming the kingdom of God. In Revelation's terms we might say that his witness drew attention to the One who sits on the throne. And being a witness to this truth about God also meant being a martyr in the sense of dying for the cause. As we shall see, the one was inseparable from the other, because to side with God is to become an enemy of the terrible dragon. Those who follow the Lamb are also called to be witnesses. Their message also proclaims the reality and sovereignty of the One who sits on the throne. And their fate will be the same as that of the Lamb.

This leads us to the other expression the elder used: "the great ordeal." Those who follow the Lamb and continue his witness in the world do so in a time of terrible hardship. The great ordeal—or "tribulation," as it is sometimes called—was predicted as far back as the book of Daniel. It refers to the time of trouble before the end of the present age. In Revelation it refers to the period from the opening of the first seal to the arrival of the triumphant Christ. In other words, it refers to the time from Christ's ascension (as the slaughtered Lamb worthy to open the scroll) to his return (as the rider on the white horse). It is the age we are presently living in. To be a follower of the Lamb is to live in a time of trouble—as Jesus himself said (Jn 16:33). I noted earlier that to have the mark or seal of God is to be protected in some sense. Now we learn that this protection is not from suffering or martyrdom. It is protection from being overwhelmed by the evil one. It is protection of our loyalty and commitment. In essence it is protection of our souls.

Revelation portrays all who follow the Lamb as witnesses/martyrs and sometimes also as "overcomers" or "conquerors." These are not titles restricted to a small elite band of supercommitted saints. They are Revelation's way of telling us that to be a follower of the Lamb is to share in his victory by sharing in his witness/martyrdom. To follow the Lamb is to do what he did, and to die as he died. This is not to say that all those who identify with Jesus will be killed for their faith, or that only those who die for their faith are true followers. Rather it means that true discipleship requires a life of self-sacrifice, a life that embraces the gospel's fundamental spiritual insight: Life comes through death and victory comes through defeat. This is what Jesus preached, and this is what he practiced in his own life. We who follow him must not expect anything different.

All of this has significant implications for how we think about what some Christians refer to as "the rapture." There are many different forms of rapture doctrine, but the basic idea is that at some point in the future, before Christ's promised return, those who belong to him will be miraculously removed from the earth. In a moment and without warning they will be snatched away from the trials and persecutions of life on earth and united with Christ in the air. Why? Because God will not allow them to experience the terrible hardships, apostasy and judgment that will come to the earth during a time of intense "tribulation" just prior to Christ's second advent.

What does Revelation have to say about this? Nothing at all! John's vision gives us no reason whatsoever to think that anything like the rapture will ever take place. To start with, rapture doctrine requires us to believe in a specific period of intense "tribulation" (usually understood to last for seven years) just before the end of the world. But the period of tribulation is better understood as the entire church age, and it has already been going on for nearly two thousand years. During every part of this period, Christians all around the world have been faithful and true witnesses to the truth about God and have paid the price for their opposition to the forces of evil, sometimes even suffering and dying for their faith. From this perspective on the meaning of the tribulation, the idea of rapture makes no sense at all. We know very well that God does indeed allow Christians to go through times of intense persecution and opposition. And if that is the case, then the rapture loses its purpose.

Revelation itself supports this. When the heavenly elder refers to those who have "come out of the great ordeal," he makes it clear that they have done this not by being raptured but by sacrificial identification with Christ. They have washed their robes in his blood. In 7:9 we read that the great multitude standing before the throne is robed in white (a symbol of both victory and purity), with palm branches in their hands (another symbol of victory). It is because they have *come through* the great ordeal that they are able to stand before God's throne in the way that they do:

For this reason they are before the throne of God and worship
him day and night within his temple, and the one who is
seated on the throne will shelter them. They will hunger no
more and thirst no more; the sun will not strike them nor any
scorching heat; for the Lamb at the center of the throne will
be their shepherd, and he will guide them to springs of the
water of life, and God will wipe away every tear from their
eyes. (7:15-17)

What is so striking about this description is that those who
stand before the throne are being comforted. They have hun-
gered and thirsted. The heat has scorched them and they
have wept many tears. They have not lived in continual hap-
piness and ease, nor have they been whisked away from danger at the last minute. On the contrary, they have washed
their robes and made them white in the blood of the Lamb.
They have come through the great ordeal. And now God himself comforts them.

What about those other passages in the New Testament
that seem to speak of the rapture? The classic example is
1 Thessalonians 4:13-18, which does indeed speak of our
being caught up in the clouds to meet the Lord in the air. But
this is not talking about "the rapture," it is talking about the
final resurrection. The moment of Christ's return will signal
the end of the present age. All those who belong to Christ
will be raised from the dead—even those who happen to be
living at the time.

This might sound like a contradiction, but it is not. Paul
makes clear in 1 Corinthians 15 that while we are alive on
earth we are mortal, corruptible, perishable. In such a state
we cannot possibly inherit the kingdom of heaven (1 Cor

15:50). However, when Christ returns we will be transformed from corruptible to incorruptible, from perishable to imperishable. This is what it will mean to experience resurrection. We will be changed from the life of the present age into the life of the eternal age. Whether we have been dead for years before Christ comes or are living at the time, we must all undergo resurrection, transformation, if we are to be with Christ.

The passage in 1 Thessalonians is saying the same thing. When Christ returns all those who belong to him will be caught up to him, an event that marks the end of the present age. No one will be "left behind" to carry on their daily activities as if nothing has happened. The return of Christ will not be a secret event that happens only in the lives of the faithful. It will be a cosmic event that will usher in a whole new day for the entire human race. The old will be completely gone; the new will be wholly here. So we should be looking forward to the resurrection that will take place when Christ returns to establish his kingdom. We should not expect a prior event that snatches us away from the trials of the present age. As long as we are in the world we will have trouble. To follow the Lamb and to be identified with him is to share his experience of the world's hatred and the dragon's hostility.

The two witnesses. The message of the first "pause passage" in chapter 7 is taken up again in the second such passage, which is chapter 11. The kernel of this section's message is a short story, almost like a parable, that portrays the role of the Lamb's followers in the coming of God's kingdom. It is a story about two people, called "witnesses," who preach a message of repentance to all the people of the earth for 1,260 days. While they do this, they are indestructible. But as soon as their task is finished, they are killed by a terrible monster that "comes up from the bottomless pit" (11:7) and their bodies are left unburied and exposed for three-and-a-half days. After that they are miraculously resurrected and taken up to God in a series of tumultuous events, including a violent earthquake and great destruction. The outcome of it all, we are told, is that those who are not killed by the earthquake are terrified and give glory to the God of heaven.

Before the story even starts, though, John is told to "measure the temple of God and those who worship there" (11:1), but he is not to measure the outer court of the temple because it has been given over to the nations to trample for forty-two months (11:2). This preface to the account of the witnesses emphasizes one aspect of their story: the people of the Lamb are protected by God even as they are being oppressed and trampled down by the forces of the dragon.

One of the keys for understanding chapter 11 is to decipher the meaning of the various periods of time that it mentions—for example, the forty-two months of trampling, the 1,260 days when the witnesses are to do their work, and the three-and-a-half days that their dead bodies will lie exposed to their enemies. What are we to make of all this? These periods refer to the great ordeal we have just been talking about. They do not tell us anything about the literal duration of the "tribulation." Rather they tell us *what the tribulation is like*. How? By recalling the book of Daniel. In Daniel we read of a blasphemous and arrogant superpower that will "wear out" God's people for "a time, two times and half a time" (Dan

7:25)—in other words, for three-and-a-half "times" (1 + 2 + $\frac{1}{2}$ = $3\frac{1}{2}$). Daniel's period of crisis was played out in the terrible events of the second century B.C., when the Hellenistic king Antiochus Epiphanes mounted a violent attack on the Jews and tried to destroy both their temple and their way of life. More than two hundred years later, John uses the concept of three-and-a-half periods of time (whether years or days) to talk about another time of terrible crisis, similar to the one in the days of Antiochus Epiphanes. The three-and-a-half years are forty-two months divided by twelve, as well as 1,260 days divided by 360 (thought to be the number of days in a year). And the slain witnesses went unburied for three-and-a-half days. Table 4.1 demonstrates these calculations.

Table 4.1

42 months: $42 \div 12 = 3\frac{1}{2}$ years
1,260 days: $1,260 \div 360 = 3\frac{1}{2}$ years
$3\frac{1}{2}$ days

Similar numbers appear elsewhere in Revelation. John sees a horrifying beast that makes war on God's people and defeats them for forty-two months (13:5). He also sees a woman (symbolizing God's people) who is threatened by the great dragon, but is protected and nourished by God in the wilderness for 1,260 days (12:6), which John later calls "a time and times and half a time" (12:14).

All these references drive home two points: that the present age is a time of tribulation and conflict; that God protects, sustains and nourishes those who are his own, even if appearances seem otherwise. This second idea has strong biblical roots. After the Israelites escaped from Egypt, they felt abandoned in the wilderness (Ex 16:2-3). In fact, though, they were being nourished and guided by God. They received manna and quail to eat and water from a rock to drink; a cloud guided them by day and a pillar of fire by night. They were attacked by enemies and wild animals, yes. They were rebellious and mutinous, yes. They grew weary of their travels and sometimes wished they had never left Egypt, yes. But in the end God did indeed bring those who held on to their faith to the place he had promised.

So it is for the followers of the Lamb. We are nourished and guided in a context of hardships and conflict. We face enemies, troubles and the rebellion of those around us. We are painfully aware of sin and apathy in ourselves. Nevertheless, to follow the Lamb is to join the company of those who accept the harsh realities of the present age, knowing that this is where we are called to worship the One who sits on the throne. We know that the way to God is through resurrection. But resurrection comes after death.

I mentioned earlier that the two witnesses are preachers of repentance. This is based on the fact that they are "wearing sackcloth" (11:3), a biblical symbol of repentance. The witnesses' role is to confront the world with the reality of God and to call on everyone to abandon their godlessness and idolatry. As worshipers of God, their task is to call on the nations of the world to join them.

The witnesses are prophets too (11:3, 10) in the sense that they speak on behalf of God. They remind us especially of Moses and Elijah. Like Moses, they can make water turn to blood and strike the earth with plagues; like Elijah, they bring fire from heaven. However, they are not Moses and Elijah come back to life, nor do they represent the Law and the

Prophets as is sometimes suggested. Rather, both Moses and Elijah are examples of individuals who opposed the evil system of their time in obedience to God and at great personal cost. In this sense they are models of what it means to be a true witness. Ultimately, of course, the two witnesses parallel Jesus. They are killed in "the great city that is prophetically called Sodom and Egypt, where also their Lord was crucified" (11:8). And like Jesus they are eventually vindicated by being raised from the dead and taken up to God. So, once again Revelation makes the point that to follow Jesus means to continue his work and share in his experience. If you choose to follow a slaughtered Messiah you should expect nothing less for yourself, because this is the way God has chosen to accomplish his purposes for the world.

Conclusion

We began this chapter by noticing that Christ is portrayed as a sacrificial Lamb, and that his victory over evil is linked to his death. He overcame Satan by bearing true witness, even to the point of death. In fact, his death is the beginning of a new exodus. Just as God rescued his people from the forces of evil in the land of Egypt, so now again God is calling his end-time people out of slavery to a new promised land. Those who follow the Lamb are like him in that they share in his victory over evil. They do this by continuing his sacrificial witness in the world. Those who belong to the Lamb follow him wherever he goes, and they wash their robes and make them white in the blood of the Lamb. This is a profound message of identification with Christ. It says that those who want to follow Jesus must be like him.

Revelation does not allow a simple equation between the
"church," and followers of the Lamb. Rather, the point is precisely that the members of the churches *must be* followers of
the Lamb. The seven messages to the churches in chapters 2
and 3 urge the Christians of Asia Minor not to be complacent,
not to compromise with the spirit of the age, not to think
they are above criticism. Christ also warns them that as their
love grows cold and as their distinct identity as followers of
the Lamb becomes blurred, they are in danger of losing their
place in his plans. Thus, he says to the church in Ephesus:
"Remember then from what you have fallen; repent, and do
the works you did at first. If not, I will come to you and
remove your lampstand from its place, unless you repent"
(2:5). To the Christians at Sardis he says, "I know your works;
you have a name of being alive, but you are dead. Wake up,
and strengthen what remains and is on the point of death, for
I have not found your works perfect in the sight of my God"
(3:1-2). And to the Laodiceans he warns, "I am about to spit
you out of my mouth" (3:16).

Added to this is a message of coming judgment: "And all
the churches will know that I am the one who searches
minds and hearts, and I will give to each of you as your
works deserve" (2:23). Revelation refuses to let us become
smug about our place in this great vision. It is not simply a
case of good guys against bad guys. When great and terrible
Babylon is eventually vanquished near the end of the vision,
we have no sooner begun cheering her downfall than we
realize that we ourselves are implicated in her defeat. "Come
out of her, my people, so that you do not take part in her sins,
and so that you do not share in her plagues" (18:4). The

church is in Babylon! That is why John's message is not just one of comfort. It is also a dire warning, urging us to see clearly the way things really are, and to decide to follow the Lamb whatever the cost. Let there be no mistake, the cost is high. To be a follower of the Lamb is to be a mortal enemy of the great seven-headed dragon. That is what we will look at next.

5

THE DRAGON

Revelation calls us to center ourselves and our view of reality on the One who sits on the throne. It is a summons to worship God. In the context of the world we live in this is an act of war because God's rule is disputed. Declaring allegiance to God amounts to deliberate rebellion against the one who is known in the Bible as the "ruler of the power of the air" (Eph 2:2) and "the ruler of this world" (Jn 12:31). John's vision confirms with stark clarity the grim truth declared by the apostle Paul: "Our struggle is not against enemies of blood and flesh, but against the rulers, against the authorities, against the cosmic powers of this present darkness, against the spiritual forces of evil in the heavenly places" (Eph 6:12).

To worship God is to respond to a battle cry. But even more than that, to worship God is to respond to a call to "Come and die!" Revelation 11:7 summarizes what followers of the Lamb can expect for their labors: "When they have finished their testimony, the beast that comes up from the bottomless pit will make war on them and conquer them and kill them." This is the "dark side" of the message of Revelation, yet it is no more avoidable than the requirement to worship God or to follow the Lamb. This is part of what it means to hear what the Spirit is saying through John's vision.

We saw earlier that chapter 11 is pivotal because it gives us, in concentrated form, what much of the rest of Revelation will spell out at greater length. It referred briefly to the conflict between the two witnesses and the "beast"; chapters 12 and 13 expand and elaborate on that conflict.

Chapter 12 is an interesting example of how Revelation uses the folktales of the ancient world to tell the story of the gospel. In both Greece and Egypt there were well-known tales recounting how a usurper or imposter tried to destroy the heir to the throne in his infancy, or sometimes even before he was born. Many modern stories follow this classic outline too. The animated film *The Lion King* is a good example. As these stories go, the usurper fails to kill the heir who eventually returns from hiding to claim his rightful place. One ancient Greek version of the story recounts how Python's attempt to kill the infant Apollos is frustrated by the child's mother, who escapes from his clutches and flees to safety. When Apollos grows up he returns to kill the dragon. In Egyptian versions the action centers around the red dragon, who attacks the pregnant Isis but is later killed by her son Horus.

These stories were themselves versions of even older Mesopotamian tales about the dragon of darkness who tried to kill the sun god, and seemed to have succeeded until he was slain by the dawning of a new day. In other words, it was a story taken from an age when sun, moon and stars were thought to be celestial beings or gods. And this is the form of the story John sees played out before him: a pregnant woman clothed in the sun and pursued by a great dragon— except that this time the story being told is really the story of the gospel. The dragon pursues the woman because he wants to destroy her unborn child who is the rightful heir to the kingdom of the world. The child is Jesus, the Messiah. The mother, we learn, is not his literal mother Mary but the community of God's people to whom the Messiah is given. The dragon, who is Satan, intends to devour the child, but the child is "snatched away and taken to God and to his throne" (12:5). The woman flees into the wilderness "where she has a place prepared by God, so that there she can be nourished for one thousand two hundred sixty days" (12:6).

The reference to the child being snatched away to God and his throne is ironic, because it refers to Christ's resurrection and ascension—events that followed his crucifixion. Those who already know the gospel story realize that the dragon did indeed kill Jesus. But what looked for all the world like Jesus' defeat turned out to be his victory because God raised him from the dead and gave him a place at the heavenly throne. His death was in fact the very event that qualified him to open the scroll and so begin the implementation of God's plan for establishing his kingdom. Here again Revelation drives home the point that victory comes through what seems to be defeat. This point is repeated with reference to the woman, or the people of God. She is driven into the wilderness, an apparent sign of her defeat, but it is actually a place of nourishment for her. The woman, like her son, suffers in order to come to God.

No sooner has the story been completed than John immediately retells it from a different vantage point and with a new emphasis. This time he sees a war in heaven between the dragon and his angels on one side, and Michael the archangel and his angels on the other. Michael defeats the dragon; he and his angels are thrown down to the earth. When this happens a loud voice proclaims, "Now have come the salvation and the power, and the kingdom of our God and the authority of his Messiah" (12:10). As the voice continues it becomes clear that the victory Michael and his angels have won over the dragon is in fact a victory that the followers of the Lamb participate in: "the accuser of our comrades has been thrown down, who accuses them day and night before our God. But *they* have conquered him by the blood of the Lamb and by the word of their testimony, for they did not cling to life even in the face of death" (12:10-11).

The human followers of the Lamb are now credited with the defeat of the dragon. However, as the voice makes clear, their victory is based on the earlier victory of the Lamb, whose shed blood makes their victory possible and becomes the energizing force in their sacrificial witness. The followers of the Lamb are able to overcome the dragon because they share in and continue the witness of Christ. The vision of war in heaven, leading to the dragon's expulsion, emphasizes the fact that the death of Jesus becomes the victory by which Jesus eventually destroys the dragon.

All of this fits well with other passages in the New Testament that link Jesus' death to victory over Satan. In Colossians 2:15, for example, we read that "[God] disarmed the rulers and authorities and made a public example of them, triumphing over them in [the cross]." And Jesus himself, when predicting his own death, said, "Now the ruler of this world will be driven out" (Jn 12:31).

Satan's banishment from heaven is by no means the end of the story, nor is it the end of his ability to do great harm to the inhabitants of the earth. While Satan's defeat and expulsion result in rejoicing in heaven, they are accompanied by a dire warning for the people on earth: "But woe to the earth and the sea, for the devil has come down to you with great wrath, because he knows that his time is short" (12:12). Thus, when chapter 12 returns to the story of the woman and the dragon, the focus is on the dragon's attempt to destroy both her and "the rest of her children." In this way Revelation again emphasizes the close connection between Christ and those who follow him. He is the woman's first son, as it were, and his followers are the rest of her offspring. Just as the dragon once tried to destroy Christ, so now it tries to destroy the followers of Christ. And just as the dragon was ultimately thwarted in its murderous designs on Christ, so it is frustrated in its attempts to exterminate his people. Using imagery that reminds us powerfully of the exodus of the Israelites from Egypt, Revelation portrays the woman being carried away into the safety of the desert on the wings of a great eagle (compare Ex 19:4). When the dragon tries to overwhelm her with a great river spewed from its mouth, the earth itself swallows the venomous flood. The Old Testament has a comparable story, with the earth swallowing up those Israelites who revolted against Moses in the desert (Num 16:31-33).

While the story of the exodus provides one level of meaning for this episode, allusions to the Garden of Eden provide another. The Greek word used for the woman's children in Revelation 12 is *sperma* ("seed"). This echoes God's words to the serpent in the Garden: "I will put enmity between you and the woman, and between your [seed] and hers; he will strike your head, and you will strike his heel" (Gen 3:15). Revelation uses the word "seed" to refer not just to Jesus (as Paul did in Gal 3:16), but to his followers as well. The woman's children are those who keep God's commandments and hold the testimony of Jesus. To be the seed of the woman is thus to become embroiled in an ancient hostility that dates back to the beginning of time. Revelation implies that Satan's initial hatred was focused on Jesus, the child of the woman, but now that Jesus is beyond his reach the full force of his fury is focused on us, the rest of the woman's children. This is one of the solemn facts of the gospel message. As 1 Peter 5:8 puts it, we have an enemy who prowls around like a lion seeking people to devour. Our response is to be sober, to be watchful, and to resist him as we remain steadfast in the faith.

The action in chapter 12 eventually comes to an end with the dragon going back to the sea. He has returned to his natural abode, the treacherous sea, for reinforcements in his war on the followers of the Lamb. This leads quickly into the next ominous chapter in which we are introduced to the beast from the sea and the beast from the earth.

Monsters from the Sea and the Land

The dragon, thwarted in its designs against both the Messiah and the woman, now sets its evil sights on "the rest of her children, those who keep the commandments of God and hold the testimony of Jesus" (12:17). Its assault is indirect, through two others that wield its power and authority: a sea monster and a land creature. Together, this evil duo mounts a concerted and unified attack on the followers of the Lamb.

The sea monster in particular has a strong biblical pedigree. Centuries before the book of Revelation was written, the seer Daniel described a vision of four beasts coming out of the sea: a lion with eagle's wings, a bear, a winged leopard with four heads, and a fourth beast with ten horns. Revelation's beast combines parts of all four. It has ten horns, it is like a leopard, it has bear's feet and a lion's mouth. Daniel's beasts represented the ancient kingdoms of Babylon, Media, Persia and the Seleucids. Revelation's composite monster is the ultimate superpower, drawing into itself characteristics from each of its predecessors. Thus what the dragon calls up from the sea represents the evil systems of the world in all their forms: political, military, social, economic and religious.

John's readers would have recognized the beast summoned from the depths of the abyss as the superpower of their own day: Rome, with her world-conquering armies and blasphemous claims of divinity. Rome was like the worst of the ancient enemies of God's people—Babylon, the Seleucids, Antiochus Epiphanes—come back from the dead. Here was a superpower that arrogated to itself honors due to God alone. Here was a force that demanded absolute allegiance and unquestioning loyalty, even veneration, from its subjects. Here was the personification of the dragon's wrath against the followers of the Lamb, the incarnation of the evil of the ages. To resist its will meant destruction, and to refuse its global agenda meant being marginalized and cut off from the sources of life, prosperity and civilization. Yet to submit to this beast would be an act of idolatry, a form of apostasy.

Even for us today, this is a key theme of Revelation's message. It is a warning not to worship power and influence, wealth and prestige. These are the beast's claims to fame. As Revelation puts it, "In amazement the whole earth followed the beast. *They worshiped the dragon,* for he had given his authority to the beast, and they worshiped the beast, saying, 'Who is like the beast, and who can fight against it?'" (13:3-4). This question is a tragic parody of the song of Moses after the miracle at the Red Sea: "Who is like you, O LORD, among the gods? Who is like you, majestic in holiness, awesome in splendor, doing wonders?" (Ex 15:11). To be cowed and overawed by the beast is to succumb to the blasphemous claims of that which is not God. Alternatively, to refuse to worship the beast is to experience its anger and fierce hostility, for "it was allowed to make war on the saints and to conquer them" (13:7).

This is not a message about what might happen in the future. It is a message about what is happening, has always happened, and will continue to happen. Revelation depicts as a time of conflict the age in which we live, the age all of Christ's disciples have always lived in. It is the time of the dragon's fury and the era of the beast's rule. As Revelation puts it, "Let anyone who has an ear listen: If you are to be taken captive, into captivity you go; if you kill with the sword, with the sword you must be killed. *Here is a call for the endurance and faith of the saints*" (13:9-10).

Those of us who live in times of peace might find this harder to believe than do our brothers and sisters who face severe persecution for their faith even now. But Revelation is for all of God's people, wherever they live and whatever their circumstances. Nor should we think that the lack of religious persecution in our land is an indication that the beast is not active here. It is, though its methods are subtle and deceptive. John's vision indicts as demonic any earthly power—be it political, military or economic—that demands absolute and unthinking allegiance. Rome was one example of such a power; there have been many others since then. Indeed, it is not just superpowers that can participate in the spirit of the beast. Institutions of all kinds—big or small, national, multinational or local—may choose to operate in this manner. Revelation warns us sternly to avoid such corruption and arrogance.

One of the most disturbing aspects of this terrifying monster is that it is also a parody of Jesus. It is a false savior, an Antichrist. In 13:3 we are told, "One of its heads seemed to have received a death blow, but its mortal wound had been healed." Two more references to this "near death" experience (13:12, 14) indicate that this is a defining feature of the beast. It has been raised from the dead. It is immortal, or so it seems to the inhabitants of the earth. And it is partly this apparent indestructibility that causes the inhabitants of the world to be so amazed by it and to worship it. The deeper truth for John's readers and for us is that ultimate evil often parades as ultimate good. Christ's victory came through death and resurrection. This beast only seems to die and be raised from the dead. Its claims to immortality are an illusion. But this appearance of indestructibility is a large part of the beast's great power. To oppose what seems invincible or inevitable is foolish; it makes more sense to compromise with the forces of oppression, rather than speak and act against them. If we believe we cannot win, we are frightened to fight at all. So fear leads to a sense of powerlessness, inertia and apathy. The inhabitants of the earth are intimidated into passivity by the dragon's great power. Only those who belong to the Lamb are able to withstand its force.

This sea beast's aura of invincibility stems partly from the work of another beast, the one that comes forth from the earth (13:11). This second beast functions like a demonic public relations consultant to the first. It is a propagandist, glamorizing and covering over the atrocities of the first beast—just as Goebbels did for Hitler in the Nazi era. Historically, this second monster stands for the imperial cult, the state-sponsored and state-enforced worship of the Roman emperor. As John says, "It exercises all the authority of the first beast on its behalf, and it makes the earth and its inhabitants worship the first beast whose wound had been healed" (13:12). Included in its bag of tricks is the ability to perform the acts of a great prophet, such as making fire come down from heaven the way Elijah did (1 Kings 18:38) along with other "signs" that deceive the earth's peoples into making an image of the beast. And its power is not restricted to the religious sphere. It has enormous financial muscle as well, so that no one can participate in the economy who does not also participate in the beast's worship (12:17). Thus, far from affirming Rome's image of itself as the savior of the world, John's vision exposes the devastating power of hell itself.

The Mark of the Beast

One of the most mysterious and chilling aspects of Revelation's portrayal of the dragon's activity is the mark that is placed on the right hand and forehead of those who follow the beast. Many interpreters have spent a great deal of time speculating about the nature of this mark and putting forward innumerable suggestions for what it might be—including bar codes on merchandise and credit cards, or computer chips inserted under people's skin. Biblical scholars, on the other hand, look to ancient practices for clues. Some have noted that *charagma*, the Greek word used here for "mark," was a technical term for the imperial stamp on commercial documents and for the imprint of the emperor's head on coins. These might explain the mark on the hand and the inability to buy or sell without the mark, but seem less helpful for explaining the mark on the forehead (though it could indicate a mind obsessed with money). Slaves were sometimes branded on the forehead with the mark of their owner—perhaps this is what we should have in mind.

Some scholars see here a parody of the instructions Moses gave to the people of God just before he died:

> Keep these words that I am commanding you today in your heart. Recite them to your children and talk about them when you are at home and when you are away, when you lie down and when you rise. Bind them as a sign on your hand, fix them as an emblem on your forehead, and write them on the

doorposts of your house and on your gates. (Deut 6:6-8)

Binding God's words to the forehead and arm symbolized their control over thought and action. They also identified the wearers as people of the Covenant. The mark of the beast might be seen to have a similar function, but with very sinister implications: those who have the mark belong to the beast and do his bidding.

Whatever the cultural background or historical precedent for the mark, its most important function is as a travesty or perversion of the seal of God that is put on the foreheads of the 144,000 followers of the Lamb as a sign of their loyalty and belonging (7:3-4). In the same way the mark of the beast is a sign of loyalty and belonging, not to God but to the beast. And just as we should not interpret the seal of God as something visible to the naked eye, so we should not think of the mark of the beast as something that can be seen, or indeed even as a physical reality. It is a spiritual mark, an attitude, a mindset that shows compliance with the agenda and methods of the beast. In the world of the beast only those who worship him can succeed. Because the followers of the Lamb refuse to take the mark of the beast, they enter into conflict with the beast's diabolical purposes and so are excluded from his economy. This makes the mark of the beast a cunning aspect of the dragon's strategy to destroy the followers of the Lamb. It is a part of his design to lure people into his sphere of influence. Thus, far from avoiding credit cards or fearing the rise of computer technology (which can, of course, be put to good as well as evil uses), we should be searching our hearts and examining the evidence of our choices and lifestyles. In them we will discern the extent to which we and our communities are either resisting or accepting the spirit of the beast in the world.

The numerical value of the mark of the beast is one of the most tantalizing features of this riddle. It is explicitly said to be "the number of its name" (13:17), and that the number refers to a specific person (13:18). To understand what John is saying here, we need to know something about the ancient practice of gematria, in which Hebrew and Greek letters of the alphabet were also used as numerals. For example, the first letter of the Greek alphabet, *alpha* (α), could stand for either "a" or 1. *Beta* (β) could be either "b" or 2, and so on, until *iota* (ι) which is either "i" or 10. After that each new letter increases by ten. *Kappa* (κ) is 20, *lambda* (λ) is 30, and so on up to 100. After that each new letter increases by one hundred. Thus any combination of letters could be a number or a word, with the result that people often took the time to note the relationship between words and numbers.

The rabbis used gematria as a way of interpreting Scripture. Hidden meanings could be extracted by comparing or linking passages with the same or related numerical values. Other ancient people used it for a code. For example, in the Sibylline Oracles (1:324), 888 indicates the Messiah because it is the numerical value of *ΙΗΣΟΥΣ*, "Jesus" in Greek (10 + 8 + 200 + 70 + 400 + 200 = 888). Christians who knew this would find their faith affirmed by the number. Gemaria was also used to satirize or poke fun at people, much like today's political cartoons.

Since we are told that anyone with intelligence may calculate the number of the beast (13:18), John clearly believed its identity was obvious. Rather than obscuring the identity of the beast, he was confirming what his readers already suspected to be true. For us, however, the meaning is difficult to decipher. A sum will result from a particular combination of numbers, but many combinations of numbers can produce the same sum. For example, 4 + 4 can only equal 8, but 8 can

Table 5.1. Gematria

Greek		Hebrew	
α	1	א	1
β	2	ב	2
γ	3	ג	3
δ	4	ד	4
ε	5	ה	5
F	6	ו	6
ζ	7	ז	7
η	8	ח	8
θ	9	ט	9
ι	10	י	10
κ	20	כ	20
λ	30	ל	30
μ	40	מ	40
ν	50	נ	50
ξ	60	ס	60
ο	70	ע	70
π	80	פ	80
ϟ	90	צ	90
ρ	100	ק	100
σ	200	ר	200
τ	300	ש	300
υ	400	ת	400
φ	500		
χ	600		
ψ	700		
ω	800		

result from 3 + 5 or 2 + 6 or 1 + 7 and so on. With large numbers such as John's "666," the possibilities are practically endless.

That said, most modern scholars think the person John had in mind with 666 was the Roman emperor Nero ("Nero Caesar"). There is a bit of a twist in the tale, though, because the numerical value of the Greek letters Νερων Καισαρ *(Neron Kaisar)* adds up to 1005, not 666. But 666 is the total when the title is written in Hebrew (נרון קסר). This might seem contrived, except that John reveals a keen interest in the Hebrew word for things in a number of other places (for example, 9:11; 16:16). Also some of his readers probably came from Jewish backgrounds, so the practice would not have seemed odd to them.

For John's original readers, this allusion to Nero would confirm other hints in the book that the beast from the sea stands for the power and malignant influence of Rome. But John's target is not just the literal Roman Empire with its literal emperors: it is the Roman Empire as representative of human power set in blasphemous opposition to God. John saw with absolute clarity the evil that lay behind Rome's bid to rule the world. He saw that followers of the Lamb should refuse at all costs to compromise with this evil power. Though it is easier to go along with the dominant ideology of the day than to stand against it, John saw that this is precisely what followers of the Lamb are called to do. He also saw that refusal to compromise would lead inexorably to all-out combat with Rome, and that this would have devastating effects on the opposition. Despite this grim prospect, Revelation called for resisting the dragon and facing the aggression and hostility of the beast. And as it called then, so it calls us today.

The Great Whore

In chapter 17 John is given another view of the terrible beast, this time described as "scarlet . . . [and] full of blasphemous names" (17:3). As before, it has "seven heads and ten horns." What is strikingly new, though, is that a woman is riding the beast. John describes her thus: "The woman was clothed in purple and scarlet, and adorned with gold and jewels and pearls, holding in her hand a golden cup full of abominations and the impurities of her fornication; and on her forehead was written a name, a mystery: 'Babylon the great, mother of whores and of earth's abominations'" (17:4-5).

This appalling picture of a prostitute riding on the back of the beast adds new depth to Revelation's depiction of evil. At its most basic level the image of the prostitute, who is drunk on fornication and the blood of the witnesses to Jesus, is a portrayal of the city of Rome. The name "Babylon" is the way the early Christians referred to Rome (see 1 Pet 5:13). This identification with Rome is strengthened considerably by depicting the woman as seated on seven mountains (17:9), a commonly known geographical feature of that city. Finally, by calling Rome "Babylon" the Christians of the late first century were saying that Rome was the same as that great enemy of the biblical past. The actual city of Babylon was the ultimate superpower and enemy of the Israelite people. Under Nebuchadnezzar, the Babylonians sacked Jerusalem and destroyed the temple.

Revelation goes even further, depicting Babylon as a pros-

titute who lures the nations of the world to her sinful plea-
sures. The city is not just a mighty military power, she also
holds out to a gaping world a universe of attractions and
allurements. She entices by the promise of wealth and shared
power. She offers herself to all who will have intercourse
with her at the price of their own souls. Thus the prostitute is
another symbol of the dangers of idolatry. The fornication
committed with her is essentially spiritual unfaithfulness to
the One who sits upon the throne. To join oneself to the prostitute is to commit an act of adultery against God.

In its own propaganda Rome depicted itself as a noble
benefactor of the world, the one whose generosity made possible a time of peace, stability and economic well-being.
John's vision insists that such benefits are illusions that
obscure the true nature of the beast. Individuals and nations
that prosper by groveling before the pretensions of Rome are
in effect taking part in a kind of gross public immorality.
John's vision calls on Christ's followers, and indeed all the
inhabitants of the world, to separate themselves from the
great prostitute. Revelation's message thus combines stern
criticism of military domination with equally damning words
about economic exploitation and self-indulgence. To be a follower of the Lamb is to have nothing to do with either of
them.

The mark of the beast allows people to pursue worldly
wealth, while those who lack the mark are not able to buy or
sell (13:17). When the great city of Babylon is finally over-
thrown, it is the merchants and sailors, those who had prof-
ited materially from consorting with her, who wail the
loudest (18:11, 15, 19). So the followers of the Lamb are urged

to separate themselves from her corrupting influence: "Come out of her, my people, so that you do not take part in her sins, and so that you do not share in her plagues" (18:4).

Conclusion

In James 4:4 we read these powerful and unsettling words: "You adulterous people, don't you know that friendship with the world is hatred toward God? Anyone who chooses to be a friend of the world becomes an enemy of God." Revelation gives us a similar message, adding a solemn warning about the dangers of being an enemy of the world. To be an enemy of the world is to be exposed to the hatred of the dragon that seeks to devour anyone who crosses its path. The task of those who follow the Lamb is to remain unflinchingly loyal to God, to bear true witness to the reality of the One on the throne. In doing so we will come up against the powers, structures, institutions and individuals that Satan uses to entrench his power over a deceived world. And because of the dragon's great power and great anger he will seem to prevail over the people of God as long as this world lasts. But what we see with our eyes and experience in this world here and now is not the whole story. John's vision assures us that we too will eventually join in the great chorus that proclaims:

> We give thanks to you Lord God Almighty, the One who is and who was, because you have taken your great power and have begun to reign. The nations were angry; and your wrath has come. The time has come for judging the dead, and for rewarding your servants the prophets and your saints and those who reverence your name, both small and great, and for destroying those who destroy the earth. (11:17-18)

To worship the One who sits on the throne and to follow the Lamb is to become locked in mortal combat with a ferocious enemy. We cannot sit back quietly, separating ourselves from the battle. We are at war. But the outcome of the fight is assured, even though we now may be oppressed and downtrodden. To be a follower of the Lamb is to be one who conquers the dragon by taking the road that leads to death, just as Christ's own path to glory passed through the agony of the cross. The lesson of Revelation is the same one taught by the letter to the Hebrews: "Let us run with perseverance the race that is set before us, looking to Jesus the pioneer and perfecter of our faith, who for the sake of the joy that was set before him endured the cross, disregarding its shame, and has taken his seat at the right hand of the throne of God" (Heb 12:1-2).

Beyond this, Revelation warns against the seductiveness of wealth and prosperity. Just as the brute force of Roman domination was softened, for some people at least, by the prospect of increased wealth, so there is a danger that the people of God will find it more comfortable and economically advantageous to live a life of quiet compromise with the beast. This is one of the most disturbing aspects of Revelation's message for people who live in the affluent West. It is all too easy, for example, to overlook the unpleasant facts about the sources of one's own material well-being, to not ask questions rather than deal with knowing that this or that item is produced by sweat-shop labor in a country that is daily ground into the dirt by a burden of poverty and debt so heavy that its people can hardly breathe. It seems impossible to live in the West in a way that does not compromise one's claim to be a follower of the Lamb. And if so, what will it take actually to live a life of integrity? What will be the cost to our families, our communities and ourselves? These are some of the disturbing questions that Revelation challenges us not to ignore.

6

WRATH &
JUDGMENT

There is no getting away from the fact that a great deal of Revelation is taken up with wrath, anger and judgment. We shudder at terrible spectacles like the great battlefield where carrion fowl gorge themselves on the bodies of fallen soldiers and horses. What could possibly be achieved by these kinds of horrors? Are they simply fear tactics meant to bully us into submission, or is there some other purpose behind them?

Even if we can discern the point of these visions of destruction and carnage, what do they reveal about the God who participates in them? Surely judgment played out in such violent terms contradicts the love and forgiveness preached by the Jesus of the Gospels. The Sermon on the Mount teaches the followers of Jesus to love their enemies (Mt 5:44) and to "turn the other cheek" to those who mistreat them (Mt 5:39). The apostle Paul teaches us never to repay anyone evil for evil (Rom 12:17). Yet Revelation seems to depict a God bent on vengeance, and the followers of the Lamb crying out for the destruction of their persecutors (6:10). At one point, people are cowering in caves and holes in the ground, longing to die if only to escape from "the wrath of the Lamb" (6:15-17). What are we to make of all this?

The first thing to realize is that Revelation is by no means alone in speaking of wrath and judgment—the theme runs through the whole Bible, the New Testament as much as the Old. Consider, for example some of the sayings of Jesus:

> And if your eye causes you to sin, pluck it out; it is better for you to enter the kingdom of God with one eye than with two eyes to be thrown into hell, where their worm does not die, and the fire is not quenched. (Mk 9:47-48)
>
> The Son of Man will send his angels, and they will collect out of his kingdom all causes of sin and all evildoers, and they will throw them into the furnace of fire, where there will be weeping and gnashing of teeth. (Mt 13:41-42)

Nor were pictures of wrath and judgment foreign to Paul or the rest of the New Testament writers. Paul proclaims: "For those who are self-seeking and who obey not the truth but wickedness, there will be wrath and fury. There will be anguish and distress for everyone who does evil" (Rom 2:8-9). The writer of Hebrews states, "For if we willfully persist in sin after having received the knowledge of the truth, there no longer remains a sacrifice for sins, but a fearful prospect of judgment, and a fury of fire that will consume the adversaries" (Heb 10:26-27). In 2 Peter we read that "the present heavens and earth have been reserved for fire, being kept until the day of judgment and destruction of the godless"

(2 Pet 3:7). The point is evident: Revelation's pictures of the wrath of God and of judgment are not unique in the Bible. They are, in fact, quite common. But how does this fit with the message of love?

The answer to that question gets us into the heart of the gospel message because it touches on God's own nature, the kind of world God created, and what is wrong with the world. We have already seen that Revelation emphasizes the sovereignty of God, his rule over the universe. It also emphasizes God's holiness and goodness. These last two attributes may be summed up by the biblical term *righteousness,* which was one of Paul's favorite words. Righteousness speaks of both who God is and of how he acts. What God does and what he makes reflect his righteousness. Thus the world itself, the universe in which we live, reflects the holiness and goodness of God—or so it should. Paul states explicitly: "Ever since the creation of the world his eternal power and divine nature, invisible though they are, have been understood and seen through the things he has made" (Rom 1:20). The psalmist said something similar: "The heavens are telling the glory of God; and the firmament proclaims his handiwork" (Ps 19:1).

But that is not the whole story. Sin is present in the world. It is not native to God's creation; it is an alien entity, an uninvited gatecrasher. Sin and evil are an affront to God and his world. Sin destroys that which has been created good. It is like a virus or a cancer. It feeds on the thing it destroys, and God will not tolerate it forever. His reaction is firm and decisive—like a surgeon who has no mercy on the disease she is trying to banish from a sick body. The Bible describes God's reaction in terms of wrath: "For the wrath of God is revealed from heaven against all ungodliness and wickedness" (Rom 1:18).

God's wrath, real as it is, does not impose arbitrary punishments. When a schoolteacher assigns after-school detention to a pupil who has not done her homework, there is no necessary link between the offense and the punishment. This is clear from the fact that the same punishment might be used for different and unrelated offences. But God's world is created in such a way that a built-in cause-and-effect relationship exists between sin and God's response to it.

Think of it as a kind of spiritual law of gravity. If you walk off the edge of a very high cliff, your action will have dire consequences. You will fall, fast! The consequences are the direct result of your action. Sin is the same way. And its consequence is to separate us from the God who is righteous and the creator of life. In the Garden of Eden God said to Adam, "In the day you eat of [the forbidden fruit] you shall die" (Gen 2:17). The first humans doubted the truthfulness of this warning; in effect, they "walked off the cliff"—and the human race has been suffering the consequences ever since. From this perspective, the coming of death was not a random punishment. It was the inevitable consequence of turning against the source of all life in the universe. The apostle Paul says that when people reject God and engage in a life of sin, God "gives them over" to the natural results of what they have chosen (Rom 1:21-32). Thus, God's anger is not peevish or spiteful. It is the unavoidable response of a righteous God to the spoiling of his world.

All this is important background for understanding the message of the gospel. In fact, it helps us understand why

Jesus had to die for our sins. Because the consequences of sin are not arbitrarily imposed punishments, they cannot just be taken away. If you see someone step off the edge of a cliff, you cannot simply pronounce her "forgiven" for her folly and expect that this will prevent her from plunging to her doom. The deed has been done and the consequences follow quickly—that is the nature of the world. The only chance the cliff-jumper has for survival is if something absorbs the impact of her fall. And this, essentially, is what Christ's death does, though in spiritual terms, of course. By dying for us he absorbed in his own body the impact of our sinfulness. As Paul indicates, God put Jesus forward as a "sacrifice of atonement" for sins so that God could rescue those who trust in him without doing violence to his own righteous character (Rom 3:25-26).

The book of Revelation depicts God's response to evil in a quite different though not contradictory way. Here God's wrath is far more graphic and violent—a deeply disturbing and thoroughly upsetting portrayal. The reason for this change is that we are no longer in the relatively straightforward world of discourse that we find in Paul's letters, but in the strange and frightening world of apocalyptic. Thus, while Paul also used images and pictures to communicate spiritual principles, John takes us to new heights of symbolic depiction. Paul speaks of God giving people over to the consequences of their sins; John speaks of God's angels pouring great vats of deadly poison onto the earth. Paul states simply that "the wages of sin is death"; Revelation speaks of demonic locusts, cosmic earthquakes and worldwide pestilence. Paul and John are not speaking contradictory messages; they are simply communicating their messages by different means.

The function of the judgment sequences in Revelation is to tell us something about God's nature and his attitude toward sin. They give us an image of the severity of God's wrath that is active in the world because of sin, but they do not function as predictors of specific future events. They speak symbolically of the presence of God's anger in the world *even now*. This is confirmed by the neat series of sevens that are a part of Revelation's use of symbolic numbers — in this case giving the sense of full or complete judgment. In the work-a-day world where we live, things rarely occur in such neat groupings. Also, many of the events in the various judgments are common aspects of human history, albeit tragic and frightening ones. War and famine and disease are always present. By using images of them, Revelation forces us to grapple with the ferocity of God's wrath and its universal scope. Perhaps most significantly of all, though, is the way the various judgments echo and replay themes and motifs from key parts of the Old Testament. This is a very important aspect of the judgment sequences, which we will look at in more detail later.

The Judgment Sequences

We are now ready to look more closely at the sequences of judgments, and after that, at the final scene of judgment, the great white throne. We have seen that the sealed scroll symbolizes God's plan of salvation. For this plan to be accomplished, what is written inside the scroll must come to life, and that means opening the seals. But these are not ordinary seals. They represent the judgment of God. Each opened seal unleashes an event or sign associated with judgment.

Actually, the seal-openings are but the first of three series of judgments: the seals, the trumpets and the bowls. We have already seen that the three series of judgments are closely related: the bowls are incorporated within the seventh trumpet and the trumpets within the seventh seal. This means that each of the three sequences ends at the same time: the end of the seventh seal-opening happens at the end of the seventh trumpet blast, which in turn happens at the end of the seventh bowl judgment. This point is driven home by the fact that John reports thunder, lightning and an earthquake in connection with all three final judgments. The only difference is that the events increase in severity, building to a crescendo of wrath and judgment before God's kingdom finally arrives. Keep in mind, too, that thunder and lightning are also associated with the throne of God: "Coming from the throne are flashes of lightning, and rumblings and peals of thunder" (4:5). This recalls the famous scene in the book of Exodus, where God comes down onto Mount Sinai and gives Moses his law, including the Ten Commandments (Ex 19:16; 20:18). So we are reminded that the judgments come from God himself and are connected to his righteousness. They represent God's response to the sinfulness of the world.

This increasing severity is found in other aspects of the judgments as well. The stormy earthquake scene becomes more and more dramatic as we progress through the sequences of judgments. The seal-openings produce judgments that impact a quarter of the earth (6:8); the trumpet blasts call down judgment on a third of the earth (8:7-12; 9:19); and the bowl judgments affect the whole world (16:3). Thus, once again we are given a sense of events building to a grand finale, which is when God's kingdom finally arrives. This is all part of Revelation's way of increasing our anticipation, even longing, for the vision of the New Jerusalem at the end of the book.

The three sevenfold judgment sequences (see table 6.1) have no clear arrangement, other than the increasing severity of the events and the fact that all three end with the storm-earthquake. Apparently the overall purpose is to overwhelm us with the sheer volume of terrible events. Catastrophe follows catastrophe in quick succession as the earth becomes more and more a place of such carnage and destruction that it is amazing anyone at all survives. On closer investigation, however, several significant lessons emerge. They involve (among other things) the plagues of Egypt, earthquakes, a burning mountain and a falling star, and an invasion and a gathering for battle.

The plagues of Egypt. Many of the judgments remind us of the plagues of Egypt in the book of Exodus, except in Revelation they are replayed with greater severity and geographical scope. Thus we find in Revelation several references to the oceans turning to blood, not just rivers as in Exodus. Darkness, hail, boils and locusts are worldwide. At one point frogs come out of the mouths of the dragon, the beast and the false prophet (16:13). In the Old Testament story of the plagues God was punishing human arrogance set up in opposition to his own claims. He was insisting that he alone is worthy of worship. In Exodus 9:13-14, for example, God says to Pharaoh, "Let my people go, so that they may worship me. For this time I will send all my plagues upon you yourself, and upon your officials, and upon your people, so that you may know that there is no one like me in all the earth." A little later God adds that the plagues are intended to "show you my power, and to make my name resound through all the earth" (Ex 9:16). The plagues in Revelation perform the very same function.

Table 6.1

Seals	Trumpets	Bowls
Military conquests	Hail and fire, mixed with blood, burn up a third of the earth.	Sores
Slaughtering	Burning mountain; sea turned to blood and a third of the creatures and ships destroyed.	The sea becomes blood; everything in it dies.
Famine	Falling star strikes the fresh water and makes it bitter.	The rivers and springs become blood.
Death and Hades: Sword, famine, pestilence and animals kill a quarter of the earth's population.	Darkness: All the celestial lights are darkened by one third.	The intense heat of the sun scorches the people of earth.
Persecution: The martyrs cry out for vengeance and are told to wait.	Locust-scorpions from the bottomless pit torture the inhabitants of the earth for five months.	The beast's kingdom is plunged into darkness.
Cosmic earthquake	Dragon-lions with serpent tails invade from across Euphrates.	Demonic forces gather the kings of the world for battle at Armageddon.
Storm-earthquake	Storm-earthquake	Storm-earthquake

In Exodus, the plagues are not indiscriminate: they affect only God's enemies, not his people. The same point is made in Revelation. Those who have the seal of God on their foreheads are protected from the demonic locusts (9:4), and the

painful sores afflict only those who have the mark of the
beast (16:2). This is a clear indication of the nonliteral nature
of the plagues depicted in Revelation. In our world, followers
of Jesus are indeed victims of earthquakes, disease and other
calamities. Being a Christian does not give a person immu-
nity from pain or suffering. Thus we cannot jump to the conclusion that the victims of a natural disaster or a terminal
disease are being punished by God. Rather, Revelation quite
deliberately uses scenes and events that will re-mind us of
the biblical plagues of Egypt, and will force us to reflect on
the underlying meaning of those scenes.

We must also remember that the plagues in Exodus made
it possible for the people of God to escape from the tyranny
of the evil pharaoh. They were the preliminary events that
enabled the people to leave their slavery. Thus, there is
woven into the fabric of the judgments a message of hope
and salvation for the followers of the Lamb (the new Passover lamb). The plagues that are coming on the world will
usher in God's salvation. After the plagues, the exodus! John
is urging his flock not to lose heart because the time for their
rescue is near. As Jesus himself said: "Now when these things
begin to take place, stand up and raise your heads, because
your redemption is drawing near" (Lk 21:28).

Terrible earthquakes. Another significant event connected
with the judgments in Revelation is a recurring earthquake.
The first one occurs when the sixth seal is opened (6:12-17),
and each of the three series ends with an earthquake (8:5;
11:19; 16:17-21). Since the meaning of the earthquake is
essentially the same throughout, we need only look at the
first to get a sense of what they are about:

When he opened the sixth seal, I looked, and there came a great earthquake; the sun became black as sackcloth, the full moon became like blood, and the stars of the sky fell to the earth as the fig tree drops its winter fruit when shaken by a gale. The sky vanished like a scroll rolling itself up, and every mountain and island was removed from its place. Then the kings of the earth and the magnates and the generals and the rich and the powerful, and everyone, slave and free, hid in the caves and among the rocks of the mountains, calling to the mountains and rocks, "Fall on us and hide us from the face of the one seated on the throne and from the wrath of the Lamb; for the great day of their wrath has come, and who is able to stand?" (6:12-17)

What are we to make of this vision? An earthquake so great that the stars are shaken from the sky is clearly something we cannot take literally. As always, the vision communicates to us in metaphors and pictures. The great earthquake of this seal-opening is a picture of God's conquest of the spiritual powers of the universe. How do we know this? Once again, we look to the Old Testament for our clue.

The book of Isaiah warns of the destruction that is about to come upon the people of the land because of their arrogance and idolatry: "Enter into the rock, and hide in the dust from the terror of the LORD, and from the glory of his majesty" (Is 2:10, 19). Revelation's picture of people hiding in holes and caves clearly echoes this Old Testament scene. And the messages of the two passages are connected as well. God is going to judge human arrogance that insists on worshipping that which is not God.

Later in Isaiah we read: "For the LORD is enraged against

all the nations, and furious against all their hoards; he has doomed them, has given them over for slaughter. . . . All the host of heaven shall rot away, and the skies roll up like a scroll. All their host shall wither like a leaf withering on a vine, or fruit withering on a fig tree" (Is 34:2-4). In the ancient world, "host of heaven" was a way of talking about celestial or spiritual powers believed to control the course of affairs on the earth. Thus, the rolling up of the sky and the falling of stars symbolize the overthrow of spiritual principalities and powers opposed to God.

Some might find it hard to accept that passages with such graphic depictions of cosmic catastrophe can have a spiritual fulfillment. But they need only take a careful look at the book of Joel, which is yet another important part of the Old Testament background for our passage in Revelation:

> Then afterward I will pour out my spirit on all flesh; your sons and your daughters shall prophesy, your old men shall dream dreams, and your young men shall see visions. Even on the male and female slaves, in those days, I will pour out my spirit. I will show portents in the heavens and on the earth, blood and fire and columns of smoke. The sun shall be turned to darkness, and the moon to blood, before the great and terrible day of the LORD comes. (Joel 2:28-3:3)

This is the passage that Peter quoted on the day of Pentecost to argue that what was happening then was in fulfillment of the Scripture. "*This is what was spoken through the prophet Joel,*" Peter said (Acts 2:16, emphasis added). It didn't matter that the moon had not actually turned to blood, and so on. The arrival of the Spirit was what fulfilled the ancient prophecy. Thus, the great earthquake in Revelation refers primarily to God's judgment of all powers that set themselves up in arrogant opposition to him. It is a reminder to us that God's rule is not limited to the earth alone. The kingdom of God will span the entire cosmos.

A burning mountain and a falling star. A great fireball falling into the earth's waters and contaminating them—that is the event accompanying the blowing of the second and third trumpets (8:8-11). First, John sees "something like a great mountain, burning with fire" thrown into the sea; then he sees a huge star, "blazing like a torch," falling into the rivers and springs of water. In both cases he uses language that echoes the words of the prophet Jeremiah about God's judgment of the superpower Babylon.

> I am against you, O destroying mountain, says the LORD, that destroys the whole earth; I will stretch out my hand against you, and roll you down from the crags, and make you a burned-out mountain. . . . The sea has risen over Babylon; she has been covered by its tumultuous waves. (Jer 51:25, 42)

Babylon was described as a mountain because of its pride of place as a power over the whole world. But God promises to throw her from her lofty perch down into the sea. She will be brought from the heights of fame to the depths of the abyss. This is a message of God's anger against human arrogance that sets itself up against him.

The message of the falling star is essentially the same. John names the star "Wormwood," a term also found in Jeremiah 9:15. John states that "A third of the waters became wormwood, and many died from the water, because it was made bitter." In Jeremiah, the Lord states, "[I am] giving them poisonous water to drink." The image of the falling star comes from even older sources. According to an ancient Mesopotamian myth, the morning star once aspired to overthrow the greater stars and claim the throne of heaven for itself. After initial successes it was repelled and eventually forced out of the sky by the sun. The prophet Isaiah used a form of this story to rebuke the arrogant pretensions of the king of Babylon:

> How you are fallen from heaven, O Day Star, son of Dawn! How you are cut down to the ground, you who laid the nations low! You said in your heart, "I will ascend to heaven; I will raise my throne above the stars of God; I will sit on the mount of assembly on the heights of Zaphon; I will ascend to the tops of the clouds, I will make myself like the Most High." But you are brought down to Sheol, to the depths of the Pit. (Is 14:12-15)

This passage has also been understood in some circles to refer to Satan, the great fallen angel. The book of Revelation sees a strong link between Babylon and the dragon, so both are possibly in mind with this image. What is most important for us, though, is to see how Revelation uses pictures and images drawn from the Old Testament to make its own message clear. God's judgment involves the overthrow of all powers, human or spiritual, that set themselves up in opposition to him.

The invasion/gathering for battle. The scenes of an invading army and a great gathering for battle are related to both the sixth trumpet and the sixth bowl. The sixth trumpet releases a demonic onslaught from across the great river Euphrates on the eastern edge of the Roman world. Romans thought of Parthia, the kingdom beyond the Euphrates, as the domain of barbarian hordes who desired nothing more than to swallow up the civilized world in an orgy of blood and carnage. In fact, the Roman legions had suffered a number of defeats at the hands of the Parthians over a period of a hundred and fifty years. Roman expansion to the east had been halted in its tracks, and this gave Rome a sense of vulnerability to attack.

Readers of John's vision who were familiar with the Old Testament would also have found in his description chilling references to biblical prophecies of invasions by the Assyrians, Babylonians and Persians. But John was not predicting a literal invasion by the Parthians or anyone else. The army he describes is an army from hell. The horses' tails are like serpents, and they have the heads of lions, which spew out fire, smoke and sulfur. John is using an apocalyptic vision of common fears to inspire a sense of something even more appalling: the world overrun by the armies of Satan. In the Old Testament God used the invading armies of pagan nations to punish the people of the land for their idolatry and wickedness. The invasion following the sixth trumpet does the same. It is the wrath of God on a world that insists on worshiping that which is not God. The real tragedy of the scene is that the inhabitants of the earth persist in their godlessness. John writes:

> The rest of humankind, who were not killed by these plagues, did not repent of the works of their hands or give up worshiping demons and idols of gold and silver and bronze and stone and wood, which cannot see or hear or walk. And they did not repent of their murders or their sorceries or their fornication or their thefts. (9:20-21)

This continued lack of repentance is the essential reason for all the judgments of the book of Revelation. And it is the situation that the Lamb and his followers have been called to change.

The invading army reappears later in John's description of the sixth bowl (16:12-16). Here the stage is set for a terrible battle that represents the culmination of the dragon's attempts to destroy the Lamb and his followers. Working in diabolical tandem, the dragon, the beast and the false prophet (the "second beast" of chapter 13) incite the nations of the earth to a showdown that, as we learn later (17:12-14), is with the Lamb and his followers. The day of battle is called the "great day of God the Almighty" (16:14) making it absolutely clear that God's kingdom is about to arrive in unprecedented power. Also, Christ himself interjects a warning near the end of John's description of the preparations for battle: "See I am coming like a thief! Blessed is the one who stays awake and is clothed, not going about naked and exposed to shame" (16:15). This warning echoes the ones Jesus gave to his disciples in Luke 12:35-40 to be prepared at all times, and Paul's to the Thessalonians (1 Thess 5:1-10). This preparedness is moral and spiritual; Revelation is not advocating that we keep a secret bunker full of food and clothing. Jesus calls his followers to live always in a state of readiness for his return, because we never know when that will be. We will revisit the theme of Christ's return in the next chapter.

The battle itself is not described with the sixth bowl; nor is it recounted with the seventh, as we might expect. Instead, John follows the seventh bowl with a return to the cosmic earthquake that destroys both the great city of the beast and the cities of the kings of the earth. Thus we see that the final event can be depicted in different ways. While the sixth bowl depicts it as a great battle on the field of Armageddon, the seventh bowl envisages it as a cataclysmic shaking of the entire created order. The lightning, the thunder, and the enormous apocalyptic hail that bombard the earth not only destroy the world as we know it, but also drive home the fundamental point that this is the culmination of the wrath of God. The seventh bowl is accompanied by the announcement from the throne that "it is done!" (16:17).

The final battle—also an earthquake—is represented by the pressing of grapes, recalling an image from Isaiah (63:1-6) and Jeremiah (25:30). John declares that "God remembered great Babylon and gave her the wine-cup of the fury of his wrath" (16:19). This is an echo of an earlier and more extensive description of grape harvesting (14:18-20). There, the grapes are thrown into the great wine press of the wrath of God; then, in an image that deliberately evokes the language of a great battle, John continues: "And the wine press was trodden outside the city, and blood flowed from the wine press, as high as a horse's bridle, for a distance of about two hundred miles" (14:20). This deliberate mixing of metaphors shows us that John is not giving a literal prediction of the future. Rather he gives us a number of grim scenarios that conjure up aspects of the Old Testament's message against human arrogance and godlessness. By reworking these images, John enhances our understanding of the wrath of God.

A Great White Throne

As I indicated earlier, we have looked at just some of the judgment scenes, but enough to illustrate Revelation's overall message on this subject. Yet to come is the final and most awesome judgment scene (20:11-15). The hurly-burly of the seals and the trumpets and the bowls is long past, leaving the singular reality of the throne of God in awesome, silent solemnity. The earth and the heavens are no more. All that is left are the people of the earth and the record of their deeds. No human being is excluded from this scene. Everyone who ever lived is there, for Death itself has had to surrender them to stand before God's justice.

The scene is that of a courtroom. Books are opened. In them are found recorded all the deeds of every human being. All people are "judged according to their works, as recorded in the books" (20:12). This moment of reckoning is vital both for the overall message of Revelation and also for the Christian Gospel as a whole. This dreadful scene—and it truly is dreadful—gives meaning and direction to the course of history. Without the prospect of a day of judgment, when all deeds and actions will be weighed in the balance of God's justice, human life would spiral down into callous cynicism. Judgment gives us the assurance that evil will receive its just desserts. Secret deeds of private malice, along with public crimes, will all be exposed. Likewise, the unsung acts of kindness and self-giving, love and bravery, will be brought to light and acknowledged by the One who sits on the throne. No deed, however grand or insignificant, will be omitted. No person, however noble or humble, will be exempted.

Some who read this portion of Revelation might object to its emphasis upon "works." Didn't Paul insist that salvation is based upon faith rather than deeds? Yes, he did, but Paul never argued that what we do is irrelevant. Rather our actions reveal the reality of our faith, just as fruit on a branch reveals the identity of the tree. In Galatians 5:19-21 he gives a long list of sinful actions born of a life opposed to God. Then he adds, "I am warning you as I warned you before: those who do such things will not inherit the kingdom of God." In his letter to the Romans, Paul made this even clearer when he said, "For [God] will repay according to each one's deeds" (Rom 2:6), and later, "For it is not the hearers of the law who are righteous in God's sight, but the doers of the law will be justified" (Rom 2:13). James, of course, made exactly the same point when he insisted that "just as the body without the spirit is dead, so faith without works is dead" (Jas 2:26). God's judgment is based on works—that is precisely what makes judgment so frightening.

Alongside the books that contain the deeds of every person who ever lived is another book called "the book of life" (20:12). This book, which belongs to the Lamb that was slaughtered (13:8), is a register of all who follow the Lamb—and the ultimate criterion that determines each individual's fate. As the judgment scene draws to an end, those who face punishment for their sins are the ones whose names do not appear in the Lamb's book of life. Thus we have in this final scene of judgment a thought-provoking paradox. Judgment is based on deeds; we must all give an account for what we have done. Ultimately, though, it is not the record of deeds but the register of those who belong to the Lamb that determines each person's eternal destiny.

Conclusion
The purpose of the judgments, so graphically and violently

depicted in Revelation, is to make absolutely clear the intensity of God's opposition to evil. Revelation portrays the One who sits on the throne as pulling out all the stops in the battle against the dragon and his minions in the world. This message of divine opposition to evil is not a tangent or distraction from the main message of the gospel—it is an integral part of it. The outpouring of God's wrath prepares the way for the coming of God's kingdom. God's rule will not be established until sin and rebellion have been dealt with. This is the meaning of the judgments in Revelation.

By using extreme images to depict God's response to evil, John forces us to come to terms with the magnitude of the problem of sin. It is not some minor issue that can be resolved by a simple, painless solution. On the contrary, it is a matter of crucial importance that requires drastic measures to resolve. Though we understand the reasons why Revelation presents the wrath of God as it does, this must not diminish the horror or the fear that the book provokes. We are supposed to feel terror and revulsion at its scenes of destruction and carnage, not so that we will cringe pathetically before God like frightened and ill-treated dogs, but so that we will actually feel some of the drama that the book is trying to communicate and take our stance of faith accordingly. Revelation does not speak to us simply on the level of our minds. It speaks to our emotions as well.

7

NO MORE TEARS

"While there's life, there's hope" is an old and true saying. It is probably just as true to say, "While there's hope, there's life." Hope is one of the most fundamental of human motivations. When we lose this sense of something better beyond our present experience, we are apt to slip into a dark pit of depression from which it is difficult to escape. The writers of the New Testament knew this very well. They sensed it deep within as they longed for something that they did not yet have. The apostle Paul sees salvation itself as something we are still hoping for because we do not yet possess it. He says, "For in hope we were saved. Now hope that is seen is not hope. For who hopes for what is seen? But if we hope for what we do not see, we wait for it with patience" (Rom 8:24-25). Paul sets "hope" and "sight" against each other because we hope for things that we do not now see, things that are not part of our present world. Thus he implies that to see the object of hope is to possess it—when we see it we have it.

John makes a similar point: "Beloved, we are God's children now; what we will be has not yet been revealed. What we do know is this: when he is revealed, we will be like him, for we will see him as he is" (1 Jn 3:2). Seeing Christ will be the same as having Christ, and being made like him. When we finally come into possession of that for which we hope, we will be transformed by it—we will become like it. Yet even now, in the time before possession, the thing for which we hope exerts its influence on us, slowly and imperceptibly shaping us into the image of what we will one day be. Thus John goes on to say: "And all who have this hope in him purify themselves, just as he is pure" (1 Jn 3:3). To hope for Christ, to long for him, is to be made like him.

Hoping requires us to see with eyes other than our natural ones. The evidence of our natural eyes often leads us to despair and cynicism about the world we live in. But the evidence that comes from faith enlivens us, strengthens us, and gives us the courage that we need to persevere. Amazing as our salvation is, it is not yet complete—a lot more is still to come. What we have now is just a down payment, a first installment on the whole gift that God plans ultimately to give to his children. Returning to Paul, we find an earthy realism in his way of thinking. Paul knows only too well what it is like to live in the grip of pain, suffering, weakness and fear. Thus his theology faces up to the realities of life in this broken world. It acknowledges that to live in this world is to experience a groaning and an aching for something better (2 Cor 5:2). Yet Paul's theology also hangs on tenaciously to the promise of God's future—a reality that has not yet fully entered the minds and hearts of those for whom it has been prepared (1 Cor 2:9). In other places Paul says that the gracious gifts of God exceed our ability to ask or even to imagine them (Eph 3:20), that the grinding toils of this life are not worthy to be compared to the glory yet to be revealed (Rom 8:18).

The life of faith is a life of hope, made possible by a decisive event in the past: the death and resurrection of Jesus. It is empowered in the here and now by the presence of God's own Spirit. But it is oriented toward the future that still awaits us. Our hope for that future pulls us forward. It gives direction and meaning to life now. It is why Paul can say, "Forgetting what lies behind, and straining forward to what lies ahead, I press on toward the goal for the prize of the heavenly call of God in Christ Jesus" (Phil 3:13-14). Hope is the leading edge of faith.

The author of Hebrews defined faith as "the assurance of things hoped for" (11:1). Thus, hope is not uncertain or vague, even though we can hardly even conceptualize what awaits us. It is something we can be sure of, as God grants us the gift of faith. It is something that affects the uncertainties of our lives, just as it did the lives of the men and women of God in the Old Testament: "All of these died in faith without having received the promises, but from a distance they saw and greeted them" (Heb 11:13). When we hope for something in the future, we are in essence arguing that the present realities of our lives are not ultimate for us because what is in the future has a stronger hold on our loyalties and sense of belonging. We are like the Old Testament saints, who "desire a better country, that is, a heavenly one. Therefore God is not ashamed to be called their God; indeed he has prepared a city for them" (Heb 11:16).

This same hope animates the closing scenes of John's vision: a city prepared by God for those who have held onto hope in the face of despair. With this image John gives us a sneak preview of what we do not and cannot yet see. But before we can even glimpse that marvelous city, two other scenes demand our attention: the rider on the white horse, and the thousand-year reign of Christ. Both are integral to Revelation's portrayal of Christian hope.

The Rider on the White Horse

One of the most distinctive elements of Christian hope is the return of Christ. Jesus promised his closest friends that he would return (Jn 14:2-3); angelic messengers repeated that assurance when Christ ascended into heaven (Acts 1:9-11); and the apostles repeated the belief frequently (for example, 1 Thess 4:16; 2 Thess 2:1-12; 2 Pet 3:3-10). Revelation introduces the theme of the return of Christ in the very first chapter: "Look! He is coming with the clouds; every eye will see him, even those who pierced him; and on his account all the tribes of the earth will wail. So it is to be. Amen" (1:7).

The theme reemerges at various points during the sequences of judgments. For example, the seventh trumpet is accompanied by the announcement that "the kingdom of the world has become the kingdom of our Lord and of his Messiah, and he will reign forever and ever" (11:15), implying that the Messiah himself has returned to establish this kingdom. Later, during the preparations for a great battle on the plain of

Armageddon, Christ interjects, "See, I am coming like a thief! Blessed is the one who stays awake and is clothed, not going about naked and exposed to shame" (16:15). Still later, the beast and the ten kings make war on the Lamb and his followers, but "the Lamb will conquer them, for he is Lord of lords and King of kings, and those with him are called and chosen and faithful" (17:14). All of this is building up to the arrival of the rider on the white horse, in a chapter that elaborates and expands on the theme of the return of Christ.

The figure on the white horse in chapter 19 is as much a part of Revelation's theme of wrath and judgment as he is of its theme of hope. His appearance represents a convergence and embodiment of the two themes. In chapter 6, when the fifth seal was opened, we were given a glimpse of the martyrs appealing to God to avenge their deaths on the inhabitants of the earth (6:9-10). The rider of chapter 19 is the answer to that cry.

One of the most instructive aspects of the battle scene in chapter 19 is the description of the rider himself (19:11-16). Most striking is the sudden change from depicting Christ as a lamb to depicting him as a mounted warrior. Yet we are left with no doubt that they are one and the same: the title "Lord of lords and King of kings" was given to the Lamb (17:14) and is now given to the rider (19:16). Significantly, this title of universal sovereignty goes all the way back to the book of Deuteronomy, in which Moses declares: "The LORD your God is God of gods and Lord of lords, the great God, mighty and awesome" (Deut 10:17)—yet another example of how Revelation indicates the divine nature of Christ.

The rider is also given the title "Faithful and True" (19:11), connecting this scene with one near the beginning of the book where Christ identifies himself as the "faithful and true witness" who addresses the church of Laodicea (3:14). This reminds us that Christ is the Lord of the church, the one who holds the church in the palm of his hand. It also reminds us of one of Revelation's central themes: Christ in his earthly life bore true witness to the reality and reign of God, even to the point of death (see 1 Tim 6:13). Now he comes not just as witness but also as judge. These roles introduce the language of the courtroom into a scene where we might have expected militaristic images—once again reminding us not to take Revelation's pictures literally or simplistically. The vision's mixed metaphors are designed to make us pause and think more carefully about the picture that is being painted for us. In this instance, Revelation is drawing on the book of Joel, where we find a similar convergence of metaphors when the nations are gathered to a battle in the valley of decision or verdict (Joel 3:1-16). *Judgment* (a legal term) takes place in the course of a *battle* (a military term). In any case, it is best not to conclude that the battle between Christ and the beast is a military one. Military language is being used metaphorically for the final showdown between Christ and his enemies.

Christ is identified also as "the Word of God," the embodiment of God's purpose. John's Gospel said that Jesus was the Word made flesh. Here Jesus is the Word come as judge of the entire world. Symbolizing the Word is the sharp sword coming out of his mouth, by which he will "strike down the nations, and he will rule them with a rod of iron" (19:15). This confirms that Christ's weapons are not military in any conventional sense, but his victory is no less complete because of that. Finally, lest we mistakenly think that these titles tell us everything there is to know about Christ, we are also told that he has a name that no one knows except he himself (19:12). We may know much about Christ, but cannot possibly grasp all that is true of him.

Besides these titles, we are given a physical description of the rider (19:12-13). We are told that his eyes "are like a flame of fire"—another reminder of the Son of Man seen walking amidst the seven lamps (1:13) that symbolize the seven churches (1:20). On his head are "many diadems," exceeding the seven diadems on the dragon and the ten on the monster, even as Christ's sovereignty and royalty far surpass theirs. He is wearing "a robe dipped in blood"—a reference to his death on the cross by which the slaughtered Lamb had conquered (5:5), and so achieved the right to implement God's plan of bringing his kingdom to earth.

Accompanying the rider are "the armies of heaven wearing fine linen, white and pure" (19:14). These are not angelic armies, but the faithful followers of the Lamb "who follow him wherever he goes" (14:4). We already know that they have "washed their robes and made them white in the blood of the Lamb" (7:14). We were also told that those who share in the battle of the Lamb against the beast are "called and chosen and faithful" (17:14), clearly a reference to the Lamb's followers. A striking contrast between Christ and his followers is that his robes are bloodstained while theirs are white. His blood has made their robes white. Their fine linen recalls their "righteous deeds" (19:8), made possible because they belong to him. Their white horses indicate that they share in the victory of their leader.

The battle scene that follows (19:17-21) is a parallel—or rather, a grisly contrast—to the marriage feast of the Lamb (19:9). The birds of the air are invited to come to "the great supper of God" (19:17) where they will gorge themselves on "the flesh of the mighty."

The highly symbolic language used to describe the rider, his followers and the battle makes it difficult to know exactly what kind of events to expect around the coming of Christ. We cannot, for instance, assume that Christ's coming will involve a literal battle on the scale of another world war. But neither should we think of Christ's coming in purely spiritual terms. Whatever events accompany the return of Christ, they will accomplish the purpose Revelation sets out. So, Revelation depicts Christian expectations for the future in terms of two great meals. One is the marriage supper of the Lamb—an image closely connected with the arrival of the New Jerusalem that comes out of heaven from God. The other meal is the horrific destruction of the armies of the beast, which are also the armies of Babylon and its harlot queen.

The Millennium

The destruction of the beast's armies by the rider on the white horse is a great climax in the story of John's vision, but it is by no means the end of it. Nor is it the end of the book's complexities or of our difficulties interpreting it. In fact, chapter 20 is possibly the most difficult in the entire book.

On the surface things seems tolerably clear: the dragon is seized and thrown into the bottomless pit for a thousand years (a millennium), after which he is let out for a little while. In the meantime John sees thrones on which are seated people with authority to judge. He also sees the martyrs: those who had not received the mark of the beast and who had died for their witness to the truth. These come to life, and reign with Christ for the thousand years of the dragon's imprisonment. This coming to life is referred to as the "first resurrection" (20:5), and a blessing is pronounced on all those who participate in it. Over these, the "second death" (20:6)—also called "the lake of fire" (20:14)—has no power at all. When the thousand years are over, the dragon is released from his prison and once again tries to deceive the nations "at the four corners of the earth" (20:8). Again there is a great battle, this time intended to destroy the city where the saints live. The attempt fails when the dragon's armies are consumed by fire from heaven. The dragon is thrown into the lake of fire and sulfur, where the beast and the false prophet have been since their defeat by the rider on the white horse a thousand years previously.

This sketch of events raises a host of very difficult questions. Here are some of the most obvious ones: Why is the dragon put in prison for a thousand years and then let out again? (Why does it say that he *must* be let out again?) How can the resurrection of the martyrs take place a thousand years before the new heaven and new earth appear? Do these people live on an earth that is still plagued by disease, natural disasters, famine, and other ills, or is the earth somehow transformed? If the people of God reign with Christ, who is in their kingdom? Why do they have to wait a thousand years before they get to enjoy the New Jerusalem? Who are the nations who live outside the blessed city and are eventually deceived by Satan after the thousand years? (And how could they be deceived at the end of the wonderful millennium?) Why are there *two* great battles: one when Christ returns and the beast is destroyed along with all the kings of the earth, then another after the millennium? Wouldn't one battle have been enough? Why couldn't the dragon have been thrown into the lake of fire at the same time that the beast and the false prophet were?

Unfortunately, these questions—and many more like them—afford few answers. It is perhaps only small comfort to know that centuries of scholarship and interpretation have failed to arrive at any solid consensus about the meaning of this short passage. It remains one of the most difficult in all of Revelation. Of course, scholars are not the only ones who have found the millennium in Revelation interesting, even compelling. Bible-believing Christians of all kinds throughout the ages have used it as the basis for a bewildering range of hopes and visions for the future.

I want to focus briefly on two categories of millennial theory. The first category sees the millennium as a period of time that precedes the return of Christ. These may be called premillennialist views—Christ's return comes *before* the millennium. Premillennialists envisage the millennium as a time of heaven on earth: Christ is again physically present and all the world enjoys the benefits of his benevolent rule. They also tend to have an extremely negative view of the world as it is now. Things are very bad, they argue, and will continue to get worse to the point when only a drastic and dramatic personal intervention from Christ will solve the world's ills.

The second broad category is postmillennialist. As the name implies, this theory posits that Christ will return *after* a long period of increasing spiritual prosperity on earth, overseen by a vibrant universal church. For such interpreters the role of Christians in the present is to live lives of spiritual integrity, evangelistic power and social concern, hence effectively binding the forces of Satan on earth and allowing God's kingdom to flourish unabated. In contrast to premillennialists, they tend to be far more optimistic about the possibility of the gradual, progressive transformation of culture and society in preparation for the return of Christ.

These two millennial views embody radically different ideas about how God's kingdom comes, or will come, to the earth. This, in turn, leads to far-reaching consequences for how each group understands the present mission of the church. For premillennialists, that mission is to warn everyone of the coming judgment of God so they can repent before it is too late. For postmillennialists the mission is to transform society by action and engagement in the political sphere.

Both views have valid and important things to say to Christians today, but both also miss the mark because they are based on an inadequate understanding of how Revelation speaks to us. They see the events in the closing chapters of Revelation as sequential. I contend that they are concurrent or *alternate* visions of the future: different scenarios depicting *various aspects* of God's future for the world. The first of these scenarios is the battle between the rider on the white horse and the beast. The second is the thousand-year imprisonment of the dragon. The third is the day of reckoning in which all people are called to stand before the judgment seat of God. The fourth and fifth are combined in the vision of the New Jerusalem, which is also the bride of the Lamb. Each scenario needs to be read as an independent unit, because each contributes distinct elements to Revelation's vision of the future of the world. When we try to harmonize them, we run into difficulties because we are treating them as if they portray a series of sequentially ordered events. When we treat them as five self-contained but inter-related visions of the future, we can learn the lessons each one has to offer and leave it at that.

Thus the first scenario is Christ's battle with the forces of oppression that dominate and abuse not only the followers of the Lamb but also all the people of the world. The rider's victory indicates the vindication of the oppressed and the coming of justice in the historical sphere. The second scenario is the imprisonment of the dragon and the thousand-year reign of the martyrs. With the source of evil removed from the world, the followers of the Lamb will live lives unmolested by the dragon and his cronies. This is a time of unhindered co-laboring with Christ, a time for experiencing the blessing of partnership with God—an aspect of life that had been lost since the first humans forfeited their regular communion with God in the Garden of Eden. This is the fruition of God's plan, the time when God's kingdom will have come to earth. The imprisonment of the dragon indicates God's intention that evil should know it has failed, that the dragon should be consciously aware of his defeat. Then, to drive home that the dragon no longer has any future in God's world, he is let out—only to be defeated in a final decisive battle.

The third scenario deals with personal responsibility for our actions. The gathering before the great white throne gives eloquent expression to the truth that God is deeply interested in the details of human deeds. He is the guardian and guarantor of the moral fabric of the universe, the one who affirms that individual acts of both evil and good will receive their just reward. The fourth and fifth scenarios (which we will explore in more detail shortly) depict the New Jerusalem and the wedding of the bride and the Lamb. These speak of yet other aspects of God's future: his personal and unmediated presence with his people, and their intimate relationship with him.

All five scenarios draw on the witness of the prophets throughout Scripture. The classical prophets of the Old Testament, such as Isaiah and Jeremiah, took the "day of the LORD" to be an historical event, a point in time when God would judge the peoples of the world. The prophets of later generations saw God's future as extending beyond the present world. Thus Daniel speaks of a resurrection from the dead for all the righteous (neither Isaiah nor Jeremiah ever spoke of resurrection.). Revelation's vision of God's future speaks of it as both historical and ahistorical: as happening within human history and outside of, or beyond, ordinary human history. Both are vital: the prophets' vision of God's righteous rule established in this world, and a wonderful new world beyond history. God's purposes for history must be fulfilled before this world comes to an end and a new one takes its place. Once it can be said *on earth* "The kingdom of the world has become the kingdom of our Lord and of his Messiah" (11:15), then this world will dissolve so a completely new one can replace it.

Thus, we must be careful about how we read Revelation. Rather than assume the millennium is a literal thousand-year period of time, we should think about the meaning of this period within the message of Revelation as a whole. Christ's victory will establish the reign of God, and those who belong to it will share in that reign by their joint rule with him. The New Jerusalem is not so much a reality that comes *after* the millennium as it is an image of *other aspects* of God's future. Rather than a clear sequence of future events, we have a series of pictures portraying the end of things in different ways. Our task is to ponder the pictures, to reflect on their meaning, and to learn the lessons of each. If we try to reduce them to a timeline or a countdown, we will find that they yield more confusion than insight. This means our vision of the future must always contain a measure of open-endedness or even ambiguity. We simply do not know the details of how everything will work out. Those who claim they do—whether based on Revelation or any other part of the Bible—must force and twist many passages to fit their preconceived ideas. How can we trust such claims?

That said, we need not wait till we have a perfect under-standing of the millennium, or indeed any part of Revelation, before we can put it to good use in our lives. History is full of powerful examples of individuals and communities who have found inspiration and a sense of hope and purpose from the picture of the millennium. The challenge before us is not so much to become experts on biblical eschatology as to become followers of Jesus who are being transformed by the visions Revelation puts before us.

The New Jerusalem and the Bride of the Lamb

When all of Revelation's frightening apparitions and puzzling riddles have passed before us and faded away, we come at last to a beautiful city set in the context of a new cosmos, a pristine universe. John says, "And I saw the holy city, the new Jerusalem, coming down out of heaven from God, prepared as a bride adorned for her husband" (21:2). This city is both the final dwelling of the followers of the Lamb, and the Lamb's bride, beautiful in her expectation of the consummation of her love. We have already seen a similar mixed metaphor in John's vision. The city of Babylon, which is also the whore of the beast, is the moral and spiritual opposite of the city of God, which is also the bride of the Lamb. And like its horrible counterpart, the bride who is the New Jerusalem exerts a strong attraction on those who see her. Yet her appeal is not corrupting. It does not dehumanize those who consort with her. It is not based on lust, violence and exploitation.

The bride of the Lamb is also parallel to the woman clothed in the sun who gave birth to the Messiah and was persecuted by the dragon (12:1-6). In both cases the woman is made up of all who belong to her. The woman clothed with the sun is the community of the Messiah. To her were born not only the Messiah himself, but all who follow the Lamb. They are "the rest of her children" (12:17). The bride of the Lamb is made up of the community of the Lamb's followers. In the wedding preparation that follows the overthrow of the beast, we gain a glimpse of her "clothed with fine linen, bright and pure," a bridal gown that is "the righteous deeds of the saints" (19:8). The bride herself is the community of the Lamb's people, but so too are those invited to celebrate the wedding: "Blessed are those who are invited to the marriage supper of the Lamb" (19:9).

These images remind us of the times Jesus spoke of the kingdom of God as a wedding feast, and of himself as the bridegroom at the wedding. In the Old Testament, God often speaks to Israel as to a beloved wife (for example, Hos 2:14-20). As elsewhere in Revelation, the picture of the bride in the closing scenes evokes strands of thought that run deep in the biblical heritage and require us to think carefully about the meaning of covenantal faithfulness. Revelation makes clear that to love the world is to be guilty of spiritual adultery against the lover of our souls, the Lamb who is the bridegroom of the church. It also tells us that to come into the presence of Christ the bridegroom is to be caught up in a relationship of intense and personal intimacy with him.

We cannot, of course, treat the picture of the city in Revelation's closing chapters as a snapshot of heaven. Like the bride, the city that comes down out of heaven from God is a metaphor rich in texture and significance. At its most basic level it speaks of the presence of God: "See, the home of God is among mortals. He will dwell with them as their God; they will be his peoples, and God himself will be with them" (21:3).

We can hardly fathom now what this will mean. What will it be like to be in the immediate presence of the One who sits on the throne? Revelation helps us begin to think about these questions by emphasizing first of all that God's presence will mean comfort: "He will wipe away every tear from their eyes" (21:4). This is a picture of affectionate intimacy. Like a little child who, in a time of crisis, has waited bravely and anxiously for her father to arrive home and bursts into tears as soon as he walks through the door, so our coming into the presence of God will be a blessed release of the emotional tension that marks life on earth. Revelation's picture is a clear acknowledgement of the pain and sorrow of human life. To be with God will be to have our hurts healed, our brokenness made whole: "Death will be no more; mourning and crying and pain will be no more, for the first things have passed away" (21:4).

To be in the presence of God will thus mean to be, for the first time, really alive! When it says "Death will be no more," Revelation is talking about much more than the simple absence of dying. It is talking about real living. The One on the throne personally assures John, "To the thirsty I will give water as a gift from the spring of the water of life" (21:6). This image is one of deep refreshment, of new life—young, vibrant, strong. "See," says the One on the throne, "I am making all things new" (21:5).

Woven into the fabric of this picture is the assertion that to be in the presence of God is to be in community. This is where we will find our sense of true belonging. The picture of the New Jerusalem is not a picture of individualistic salvation. Using terms that recall when God made his tabernacle with the people of Israel during their wilderness wanderings, the angelic voice proclaims: "See the home of God is among mortals. He will dwell [literally, set up his tent] with them as their God" (21:3). Such language reminds us of God's covenant commitment to the people of Israel (compare Lev 26:12). Only now, this commitment broadens to include all nations: "They will be his peoples [plural] and God himself will be with them" (21:3). And again a little later: "Those who conquer will inherit these things, and I will be their God and they will be my children" (21:7).

In the paragraphs that follow, John elaborates on the image of the city in order to drive home these basic lessons about our hope. As always, he piles image upon image and picture upon picture so that we are almost overwhelmed, trying to imagine the details of the vision. This is precisely John's aim because what he describes, he tells us, reflects the glory of God. The same precious substances that featured prominently in his description of the One on the throne at the very beginning of his vision are present again here. The city radiates the glow of jasper, crystal, gold, emerald and a treasury of other jewels. Above all, John wants to give us a sense of the stunning beauty of what he saw. It is the very beauty of God himself.

Also built into this vision is the symbolic value of the number twelve, which is a reminder of the people of God, understood as the twelve tribes of Israel. Twelve is repeated over and over in the city's attributes. It has twelve gates with twelve attending angels. On the twelve gates are inscribed the twelve tribes of Israel. The city has twelve foundation stones on which are inscribed the names of the twelve apostles of the Lamb. The very dimensions of the city reflect the symbolic value of twelve. It is a perfect cube. Its height, length and width are all twelve thousand stadia (a detail obscured by the NRSV and other translations, which give modern equivalents such as 1,500 miles). The wall of the city is 144 (12 x 12) cubits wide. All of this corresponds to the number of followers of the Lamb: 144,000 (12 x 12 x 1,000).

Revelation's quite simple message is that those who follow

the Lamb belong in this city—it is for them. Revelation also notes that the gates of the city point in the four directions of the compass, reminding us again that the people of the Lamb are not to be defined in narrowly nationalistic terms. Rather, they come from every tongue and tribe and people and nation. As John tells us a little further on, the light of the city is for the nations to walk by (21:24).

John also tells us that the city has no temple (21:22). This is surprising at first, but makes perfect sense when we think about it. The ancient temple was a place where people went to meet God by carrying out religious transactions with the help of the priestly class who brokered access to the divine. Because the New Jerusalem is a symbol of God's immediate presence, the need for religious brokerage or mediation is gone, as is the need for special places and special transactions to connect us with God. The Lord God Almighty is himself the temple, John says (21:23). To be in the city is to be in the holiest place.

The city is also a place of unending light. Because God himself and the Lamb are the light of the city, there will never be any dimming of the day. This is not to consign us to an eternity in a dazzling jewelry box with no way of softening the lights. When John says, "They need no light of lamp or sun, for the Lord God will be their light" (22:5) he is talking about God's presence. The city will be the place where God himself is—and we will be there too.

As John's amazing vision enters its final moments, elements of a garden within the city emerge. There is a stream called the river of life. It is as bright as crystal and flows from the throne of God and of the Lamb. This river is related to the crystal sea John saw in his first view of the heavenly throne; it is quite distinct from the earthly sea that represents the abyss. One of the first things John says about the new heaven and earth is that "the sea was no more" (21:1). The earthly sea is the place where the dragon lives. It is the home of the sea beast that makes war on the followers of the Lamb. The absence of "the sea" in the New Jerusalem means that evil is banished—as John will say later, "Nothing accursed will be found there any more" (22:3). The earthly sea speaks of realities that parallel the other evil domain, the abyss; the river of life flowing with crystal clear water speaks of vitality, fruitfulness and healing. These are also implied by the tree of life that John sees growing on the banks of the river. It is always fruitful and its leaves contain profound curative properties (22:2). This draws our minds back to the beginning of the human story in Genesis. The tree of life was there in the Garden of Eden, but access to it was denied from the moment of the first humans' sin. The tree of life in the New Jerusalem is once more available to all. The world has come full circle.

John closes his description of the vision by restating the main quality of the city from heaven, "The throne of God and the Lamb will be in it," followed by the only possible response: "and his servants will worship him" (22:3). Thus the celestial celebration of God that John first encountered when he was summoned through the open door into heaven continues in the new world forever and ever. And those who are there "will see his face, and his name will be on their foreheads" (22:3-4).

Epilogue

As we come to the end of this short book, I am only too aware that there is still much to be said. Many passages and scenes we have not studied at all; others have been treated only briefly. Some important questions have been addressed and perhaps answered, but the answers may have simply raised new questions. This is a signal that our journey into Revelation has just begun, and an invitation to forge on further. Even so, I have tried to get at the heart of Revelation, to express the core of the book's message. What is Revelation really trying to communicate about God, and what does it mean to worship him?

God is pictured as the One to whom all creation owes its existence; his will is the ground and basis of all that *is*. The world depends on God, belongs to God, and is for God. He alone may be depicted as sitting on the throne of the cosmos. To worship God means to know all this, not just in a one-dimensional intellectual way, but with our whole beings. To worship God is to live with a deep personal sense of God's absoluteness and our dependency. This leads to an awe and gratitude that are not just mental attitudes but practical qualities to be expressed in the down-to-earth events of our everyday lives. And here, too, Revelation gives us much insight, because worshiping God is not primarily about church services or liturgies and rituals. Worshiping God is about alignment, loyalty, obedience. God's actions call out a challenge to us: Embrace or reject.

Revelation depicts God's work in the world through Scripture's most perplexing image: the slaughtered Lamb. In doing so it announces with clarity and directness that God's way of being present in the world is through weakness and suffering, through defeat and sacrifice and service. This, of course, is the great challenge that stands before us. This is the hurdle we are called to overcome. It is the stone that many people stumble over. Will we identify ourselves with the Lamb? Will we accept this sign of meekness and humility, or will we seek a more robust, more powerful image? Will we follow the Lamb wherever he goes?

But where does the Lamb go? Where does his path lead? This is another of Revelation's disturbing and unsettling lessons. The way of the Lamb leads to conflict, because God's claim to absolute rule of the universe is contested on every side. To make oneself a friend of God is simultaneously to make oneself an enemy of the world—or even more to the point, an enemy of the dragon. The dragon in Revelation symbolizes God's great enemy, Satan, whose energy is spent entirely on pursuing and trying to destroy first the Messiah and then the people of the Messiah. The vision counsels us to consider the cost of associating with Christ. It also counsels us to consider another cost: the cost of not associating with Christ.

The dragon is active in the world through its surrogates:

political, economic and religious tyranny. It is present in every temptation to worship that which is not God. Thus no part of human life is unaffected by the dragon's strategies, and the followers of the Lamb are daily faced with the knowledge that they are part of an all-encompassing conflict with a mortal enemy. This is not to say there is no rest from hardships. There certainly is. Much of the time it may even seem that the cosmic battle of Revelation is far away and irrelevant to us. But we must not let the appearance of peace lull us into a false sense of security. The battle is real, it is everywhere, and it continues unabated. Indeed, Revelation affirms that to follow Christ is to never be completely out of reach of the dragon's hatred.

This need not terrify us. Revelation also speaks of the seal of God, which distinguishes the followers of the Lamb from the followers of the beast. God knows those who are his and is working to bring them finally to the new world that John's vision reveals. But in the meantime, we live in a world that is not only the stomping ground of the dragon, but is also the sphere of the wrath of God. It is a world caught up in a complex web of the consequences of its own many sins. To be a follower of the Lamb is to be given the insight and the power that we need to live in a way that brings redemption and hope into the world. It is to live in the world as Jesus himself lived.

All these lessons have been gleaned from Revelation without treating it as a predictor of the future. We have not asked Revelation to give us information about how the world will end, or when Christ will return, or who the "Antichrist" will be. Rather we have tried to listen to this book in the terms in which it asks to be heard: as a letter written in the second half of the first century A.D. to a group of churches in the Roman province of Asia. These were real people facing real issues, and Revelation spoke to them in ways that they understood and could relate to. Our understanding of the message of Revelation today must draw deeply on what its message was to those first readers of John's amazing visions.

Revelation also asks to be heard as an apocalypse—a document written in a style once commonplace and well understood, but now strange and often perplexing. It is a work of profound images drawn especially from the Old Testament but also from the culture and history of the ancient world. It is a work of stunning sensory power, at times able to overwhelm us, to terrify us, and to move us to tears of longing. Most of all it confronts us with a challenge to worship God in company with the Lamb and in opposition to the dragon and his horde.

Revelation often seems to raise more questions than it answers. Much of it causes us to ponder and reflect deeply, yet still leaves us without firm conclusions. This is part of the purpose of the book. It is an invitation to the mystery of God in the world.

Jesus told his disciples, "To you has been given the secret of the kingdom of God, but for those outside, everything comes in parables; in order that 'they may indeed look, but not perceive, and may indeed listen, but not understand; so that they may not turn again and be forgiven'" (Mk 4:11-12). The scandal of these words applies equally to the Revelation given to John. Seven times he was told to call out, "Let anyone who has an ear listen to what the Spirit is saying to the churches" (2:7, 11, 17, 29; 3:6, 13, 22). Only when we hear and respond will the blessing of the book be ours.

"Blessed are those who hear and who keep what is written in it; for the time is near" (1:3).

Suggestions for Further Reading

The literature on the book of Revelation is truly enormous. Below is a selective list for those who want to explore further some of the ideas we have discussed in this book. I found all these works helpful, though I do not necessarily agree with every detail of their interpretation of Revelation.

For a very helpful overview of the message and genre of Revelation, see R. Bauckham, *The Theology of the Book of Revelation* (Cambridge: Cambridge University Press, 1993). For a more scholarly discussion, see Bauckham's essays on various aspects of Revelation, *The Climax of Prophecy: Studies on the Book of Revelation* (Edinburgh: T. & T. Clark, 1992).

For a comprehensive commentary from an evangelical point of view—along with lots of practical insight—see C. S. Keener, *Revelation*, NIV Application Commentary (Grand Rapids, Mich.: Zondervan, 1999). For much more detail plus extensive scholarly and technical discussion, see D. Aune, *Revelation*, Word Biblical Commentary, 3 vols. (Dallas: Word Books, 1997-1998) or G. K. Beale, *The Book of Revelation. A Commentary on the Greek Text*, NIGTC (Grand Rapids, Mich.: Eerdmans, 1999).

Other helpful commentaries that look at Revelation from a

variety of perspectives include D. L. Barr, *Tales of the End: A Narrative Commentary on the Book of Revelation* (Santa Rosa, Calif.: Polebridge, 1998); G. B. Caird, *A Commentary on the Revelation of St. John the Divine* (London: A. & C. Black, 1966); C. Rowland, *Revelation* (London: Epworth, 1993); E. Schüssler Fiorenza, *Revelation: Vision of a Just World* (Minneapolis: Fortress, 1991); and J. P. M. Sweet, *Revelation*, Pelican Commentaries (London: SCM Press, 1979).

For further information on the literary genre "apocalyptic," see J. J. Collins, *The Apocalyptic Imagination: An Introduction to Jewish Apocalyptic Literature*, 2nd ed. (Grand Rapids, Mich.: Eerdmans, 1998); and C. Rowland, *Open Heaven: A Study of Apocalyptic in Judaism and Early Christianity* (London: SPCK, 1982). For information on Revelation's use of historical allusions and mythology, see A. Y. Collins, *The Combat Myth in the Book of Revelation* (Missoula, Mont.: Scholars, 1976); and J. M. Court, *Myth and History in the Book of Revelation* (London: SPCK, 1979). For an excellent study on the seven churches in their historical context, see C. J. Hemer, *The Letters to the Seven Churches of Asia in their Local Setting*, 2nd ed. (Grand Rapids, Mich.: Eerdmans, 2001).

Index

Abraham, promise to, 75
Alpha and Omega, 59–61
antichrist, 97
Antiochus Epiphanes, 45, 83
apocalypse, Revelation as an, 28–36, 152
apocalyptic, structure of, 35–36
Armageddon, 125, 117, 133
authorship of revelation, 24
Babylon, 86–87, 95, 104
battle, gathering for, 122–25
beast from the land, 98–99
beast from the sea, 95–98
book of life, 127
bowls of wrath, 49–50, 115
bride of the Lamb, 141, 143–48
burning mountain, 121
complacency, warnings against, 44, 86
deity of Christ, 60–61, 64–65, 133
Domitian, 26, 57, 62
dragon, the, 11, 16, 150–51
    conflict with, 12, 16, 17, 38, 89–94, 103–4,
    107, 150
earthquake, 118–21, 124–25
elders, the twenty-four, 56–57
exodus, the, 70–72, 83–84, 85, 93–94, 118
fallen star, 121–22
following the Lamb, 11, 16, 17, 38, 72, 73–
    87, 135, 150
forty-two months, 82–83
futurist approach to Revelation,
    21–22, 38–39
Garden of Eden, 94, 140, 147–48
gematria, 101–3
genre, 19–39
grape harvest, 125
great white throne, 125–27, 140, 141
he who is and who was and who is to
    come, 61
he who sits on the throne, 11, 12, 15, 16,
    45–46, 51–53
historical circumstances of writing Revela-
    tion, 26–28
historicist approach to Revelation, 20–21
hope, 129–32, 133
imagination, importance of, 36–37
imperial cult, 26, 98
invasion, 122–25
judgment, 25, 46, 49–50, 73, 109–28, 133
lake of fire, 137
Lamb, the, 11, 31, 32, 67–73
letter, Revelation as a, 22–28, 152
letters to the seven churches, 44–45, 86
Lion of Judah, 69, 75
literal versus nonliteral interpretation, 29–
    30, 118, 119, 134
literature, Revelation as, 36, 58
living creatures, the four, 57–59

Lord God the Almighty, 61–62
mark of the beast, 99–104, 105
martyrdom ,76, 77, 78
millennium, 136–42
Mount Sinai, 54, 70, 115
Nero, 27, 103
New Jerusalem, 17, 141, 142, 143–48
numbers, symbolic, 25–26, 30–31, 32, 74–
    75, 146
    666, 99–104
    1,260 days, 82–83
    144,000, 73–81, 146
Old Testament, use of in Revelation, 31–32
overview of Revelation, 41–50
parody of Christ, 97–98
Passover, 69, 118
persecution of Christians, 26, 27, 44
plagues of Egypt, 71, 116–18
postmillennialism, 139
premillennialism, 138–39
propaganda, Roman, 34, 98, 105
prophecy, Revelation as, 24, 38–39, 43
rainbow, 53
rapture, 78–81
recipients of Revelation, 24–26, 44
repentance, 84
resurrection, 80–81, 84, 137, 141
rider on the white horse, 132–36, 140
robes washed in blood, 76, 79, 80
Rome, 95, 97, 103, 104
root of David, 69
Satan, 122, 150
scroll, the, 46, 67–68, 70, 114
sea, the, 54–56, 148
seal of God, the, 74, 151
seal-openings, 46–48, 115
seven spirits, 29, 31–32
source of Revelation, 43, 44
strength in weakness, 17, 72, 78, 91–92
symbolic language, 29–30, 32–35
temple, 82
three and one-half days/times, 82–83
thunder and lightning, 54
time, times and half a time, 82–83
tribulation, the great, 77–81, 82,
    83–84, 96
Trinity, 43
trumpet blasts, 48, 115
war in heaven, 92–93
wealth, seduction of, 107
whore, the great, 34, 104–6
witness, 17, 38, 77, 78, 85, 92, 134
witnesses, the two, 81–85
woman clothed in the sun, 90–94
worship, 11, 12, 15, 16, 39, 45, 51–52, 57,
    58–59, 62–65, 67, 89, 116–17, 148, 149–50
wrath of God, 109–14, 151